HOME SCHOOLS: An Alternative
You do have a choice!
by Cheryl Gorder

BOOK REVIEWERS HAVE APPLAUDED THIS BOOK:

"Home Schools: An Alternative provides valuable encouragement for those parents who want to assume the responsibility for their children's education."
—HOME EDUCATION MAGAZINE

"This is one good little book. Author Cheryl Gorder coolly and logically presents what home schooling is, why people do it, and why we should be allowed to do it....Wonderful for convincing yourself or others that home schooling is OK."
—NEW BIG BOOK OF HOME LEARNING by Mary Pride

"The legal aspects are covered very well...Documented cases are cited and terminology explained for the benefit of parents who may come up against such in the future...The real meat, however, lies in Chapter 12. It alone, with its ideas, plans, addresses, learning materials, and other resources, would make this book invaluable to any parent undertaking the home education of their children....Find the thoroughly professional, motivating contents of the author."
—PARENTS & TEACHERS OF GIFTED CHILDREN

"How did something like home schooling metamorphose from a radical reaction against the establishment into a grassroots, mainstream movement? Cheryl Gorder's book is helping in untangling the threads of this metamorphosis. What makes a home schooling parent tick? Cheryl Gorder's book gives clear answers to these questions."
—THE LIGUORIAN

"This book is written to answer the many questions surrounding today's home-schooling movement in the United States. It is for a general audience and covers a variety of topics ranging from the religious and moral issues for home schools to the legal and educational issues raised by the movement."
—MARRIAGE & FAMILY LIVING

Additional reviews in *Booklist, Library Journal, Small Press Book Review, The Family Learning Connection, The South Dakota Magazine, Homesteaders News, and many more.*

D0840265

Home Schools: An Alternative (4th edition)

Published by:

BLUE BIRD PUBLISHING
2266 S. Dobson, Suite #275
Mesa AZ 85202
(602) 831-6063
FAX (602) 831-1829
Email: bluebird@bluebird1.com
Web site: http://www.bluebird1.com

© 1996 by Cheryl Gorder

ISBN 0-933025-47-5
$12.95

Cover by Robin Graphic Designs

Library of Congress Cataloging-in-Publication Data

Gorder, Cheryl, 1952-
      Home Schools : an alternative / by Cheryl Gorder. -- 4th ed.
        p.   cm.
      Includes bibliographical references and index.
      ISBN 0-933025-47-5
LC40.G67 1996
649'.68--dc20   96-17362
                                        CIP

INTRODUCTION

If not me, who?
If not now, when?

Einstein (echoing Hillel)

Parents need to ask themselves those questions. They have to set their priorities, and then live by them. A lifestyle is hypocritical if family life is considered important, but then the family spends little time together.

My intent in this book is to help people think about their lifestyles, values, and priorities, not only in their choice of educational style, but beyond that. People have to be able to think analytically about their choices, and about the institutions around them, so that when they make a choice, it's because they have truly chosen it, not because "everyone else is doing it."

Did you stop to ask the following when your child became school-age:

Who will be teaching him?
How will he be taught?
Why will he be taught that way?

If your answer is "NO," then your child probably is not receiving the education he deserves.

Do you shop for clothing, or merely buy clothes? Do you go into a restaurant and let them serve you anything they have, or do you expect a menu? Do you select a babysitter, or do you let just anyone take care of your child?

Isn't your choice in your children's education just as important?

YOU DO HAVE A CHOICE!

C. G.

Notes about New Fourth Edition

Since the first edition of this book was published in 1985, remarkable changes have been happening to homeschooling. No longer is it seen as a strange, offbeat thing to do. Now it is becoming acceptable and even mainstream to choose home-schooling.

This alternative is so widely acknowledged as an exceptional way to educate your children that one woman told me she thought homeschoolers might now be considered "elitists." That made me chuckle, because I remember the days of homeschooling my daughter, when it was almost "weird" to do so. We have come far enough for people to consider it an elitist movement—what a transformation has taken place in the last few years!

The reasons people choose homeschooling has been changing as well. In 1985, 75% of the people choosing homeschooling were doing so for religious reasons. Today, that is about 50%, and the other 50% are choosing it as a reaction against the public schools. The segment choosing it because public schools are failing is the fastest growing part of the homeschooling population.

Parents are very upset with the violence and drug use associated with the schools. Hillary Rodham Clinton points out in her 1996 book, *It Takes a Village,* that 135,000 children take guns to school every day!

Parents are also upset that schools fail to teach children the basics of education. *U.S. News & World Report*, April 1, 1996, stated, "Only a third of twelfth graders mastered rigorous reading passages by the respected National Assessment of Educational Progress . . . The general standards of U.S. schools pale in comparison with those of other industrialized nations. Says Albert Shanker, president of the American Federation of Teachers: 'Very few American pupils are performing anywhere near where they could be performing.' " Homeschoolers find that they are able to provide a quality education better than the public schools.

Changes have been made in this edition of the book to reflect the changing status of homeschooling. Previous editions contained a chapter entitled "Harassment vs. Cooperation" which has now been deleted because the information was more appropriate 10 years ago than it is today. A new chapter has been added, "Frequently Asked Questions About Homeschooling."

I'm proud to be part of this phenomenal trend, and I still feel very strongly that:

> ## The leaders of tomorrow will be the homeschooled children of today!

For updates on homeschooling, please visit our Web site:
http://www.bluebird1.com

TABLE OF CONTENTS

ACKNOWLEDGMENTS

Special thanks to all of the people who agreed to interviews and filled out questionnaires. Hundreds of home schooling parents and also educators were a part of this book. Personal thanks to Donald & Kathleen Budke, Ed Nagel, and Jill Mociun.

My daughter, Sarah, deserves an extra pat on the back for her help in the research and editing of this book, but mostly for her enthusiastic help and encouragement for this project.

Excerpts from *Alternatives in Education*, a newsletter: "Recurring school dreams" and "Letter from Berkeley Ph.D."

Data for graph of number of home schoolers (Chapter One) provided in part by the National Association for the Legal Support of Alternative Schools, Ed Nagel, director, by Ted Wade, author of *Home School Manual,* and by the Home School Legal Defense Association.

Reagan's letter reprinted from *The Parent Educator and Family Report*, a newsletter of the Hewitt Research Foundation, Washougal WA.

South Dakota minister's letter used by permission of Rolly Wieczorek, Mt. Vernon, SD.

Gustavsen's dissertation quoted with his permission.

Family Circus cartoon used by permission of King Features Syndicate.
Gary Brookins' cartoon used by permission of *Richmond Times-Dispatch.*

Cathy Duffy's letter used with her permission.

Thanks to EVAN-G for providing updated information on corporal punishment in the schools.

ABOUT THE AUTHOR

Cheryl Gorder comes from a family of professional educators. Her father was a university professor and her mother an elementary school teacher. Cheryl herself was always a superior student. Straight "A's" were her typical grades. In fact, she graduated from high school as number one in her class of 210 students and graduated from college with high honors.

Cheryl had always planned to become a teacher, but during her education courses, she found that her ideas about public education were changing. Years later, while working on her MBA degree, she found that her ideas on public education were still in a state of flux.

She began home schooling her daughter because of extensive traveling, but soon found that there were other compelling reasons to home school. These ideas became the foundation of this book.

Sarah thrived with home education. At fifteen, she began college. She has been an "A" student at Arizona State University, and has participated in many extraordinary experiences. She had an internship at the Smithsonian Institution in Washington, D.C., working with world-reknown experts in her field of archaeology. She has studied in Kenya, Africa at the famous Koobi Fora field school conducted by Harvard.

Cheryl has continued writing and editing books. Her other books include *Green Earth Resource Guide; Multicultural Education Resource Guide; Home Business Resource Guide* and *Homeless: Without Addresses in America*, which won a prestigious Benjamin Franklin award in 1989. She is currently working on curriculums for homeschoolers.

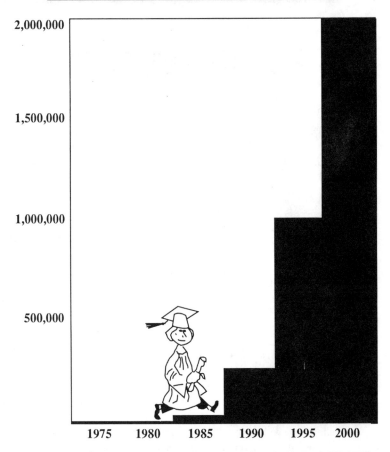

ESTIMATES OF HOME SCHOOLING FAMILIES IN THE UNITED STATES

Figures from 1976 to 1984 supplied by the National Association for the Legal Support of Alternative Schools. Figure for 1989 supplied by Ted Wade, author of *The Home School Manual.* Estimates for 1996 and 2000 supplied by Home School Legal Defense Association.

Homeschooling has been growing tremendously since the 1970s. In 1980, there were only about 25,000 homeschoolers in the United States. By 1984, the number had reached 50,000, and in 1990, there were 150,000 homeschoolers. Ever since that time, the growth has been enormous, with the number of homeschoolers increasing by at least 25% a year, and doubling in number every 4 years. At this rate of growth, there will be 2,000,000 homeschoolers in the United States by the year 2,000.

CHAPTER ONE
Home Schools: The Alternative

George Washington, Abraham Lincoln, Woodrow Wilson, Thomas Edison, Winston Churchill, Agatha Christie, Margaret Mead, Charlie Chaplin, Albert Schweitzer, Thomas Jefferson, Albert Einstein, Andrew Carnegie, General Douglas MacArthur, Charles Dickens, Samuel Gompers, John Philip Sousa, and Mark Twain.

All of these notable people were home schooled before it was controversial or, as it used to be in some states, illegal. Now home schooling is appealing to a growing segment of Americans who are dissatisfied with public schools for one reason or another.

Traditionally, the alternatives to public education have been private schools, parochial schools, and privately-hired tutors. The parents who preferred a concentrated moral and religious training combined with education chose parochial schools, if they could afford the tuition. Private tutors were hired to teach child actors and handicapped children who could not attend regular school. All of these alternatives were socially and legally acceptable.

Alternatives in public education have expanded since the 1960s. A few of the more recent varieties have been Montessori schools, behavior modification schools for delinquents, accelerated schools for gifted students, schools for pregnant adolescents, schools for the performing arts, as well as the rapid development of back-to-basics schools.

These types of alternative schools have generated controversy, but significantly little research. The fact that these schools exist, however, is proof enough that response is being made to pressure for alternatives to public education.

HOME SCHOOLS: An Alternative

The growing demand for change stems from the liberal social movements of the 1960s. Critics of public education, such as John Holt, have become numerous. In response to criticism, and to fulfill the needs of a heterogeneous society, new alternatives have been developing for the past 20 years. Most of the alternatives have been schools oriented for specialized groups, such as the handicapped, the gifted, the pregnant, and the disciplinary problem.

Now a new trend in education has rocked the premises of modern education. That trend is home schooling, or education at home by parents. Called "the educational movement of the century" by Val Canon, organizer of the National Council of Parent-Educators, the movement is gaining momentum. No longer "in the closet," home schooling has come into the public limelight. *Megatrends* author John Naisbett found that home schooling is part of the trend away from reliance on American institutions.

John Holt once advised parents to try to change the schools. Many parents, such as those who formed the Parents of Minnesota organization, tried to do just that. When they made no progress, they removed their children from public schools and began teaching them at home. Although Mr. Holt died a few years ago of cancer, his newsletter, *Growing Without Schooling*, (address in Chapter 12 and in the Acknowledgments) is still one of the forces propelling and advising the movement.

Many proponents of home schooling have appeared on national television, such as "The Donahue Show." They also have been heard on radio broadcasts and read about in newspapers. Some home schooling families have attained fame, such as the Colfaxes of California, whose sons have attended and graduated from Harvard after being taught in rural California in a very untraditional manner. The family now has a book, *Homeschooling for Excellence,* and has been seen on national television and in such magazines as *Parade Magazine*, July 17, 1988.

No longer are parents satisfied with limitations on choices. They want to be in full control of their children's education, even to the point of committing themselves to the task.

"No one knows better than me what's best for my child," is a phrase repeated over and over by parents. One by one they are pulling their children from public schools and placing them under home instruction. They are asserting their rights as parents and are becoming determined to be solely accountable for their children's education.

Many of the proponents of home education are, surprisingly, professional educators. Elizabeth Walsh of California said, "From my experience with home schooling, I see it as a positive, viable alternative to public schools and an avenue of rich, many-faceted and unlimited educational opportunities."

Jackie Sipe of Tucson, Arizona, a former third-grade teacher, said she is going to keep her child out of the public school system because, "I can monitor her social behavior much better."

PROFILE OF HOME SCHOOLERS

What kind of parents choose to educate their children at home? What reasons do parents give for pulling their children from public and private schools?

A study by Dr. Gunnar A. Gustavsen of Andrews University in Michigan detected similarities in the parents who choose home schooling. The husband is generally a professional or semi-skilled worker, earning from $15,000 to $20,000 a year. (These are 1981 figures.) Most of these parents live in small towns and typically have two children. The mother usually assumes the primary responsibility of teaching. Our sales of home schooling books over the past few years indicate that these observations hold true. Most of the letters and orders we receive are from rural areas. A handful come from suburban areas, but very few from cities. And it is usually the mother writing the letter, requesting help in starting home schooling.

The most obvious differences among the parents, Dr. Gustavsen observed, are their diverse religious and political backgrounds. Overall, home schoolers are politically conservative but individualistic, law-abiding churchgoers with one to three years of college education. Their home is very child-centered. They are average socializers and travel occasionally.

The profile of home schoolers shows them to be very normal people, different only because they are determined to provide the kind of education that they believe their children should have. Debbie Jones of Idaho summarized the feelings of most parents when she said, "I think it ought to come to light that people who do home schooling aren't weirdos or backwards hermits. We're just doing what we think best for our children."

There are different types of parents in relationship to their involvement with schools. Some are supporters but not actively involved, some are volunteers for PTA and extracurricular activities, some are volunteers for academic assistance, some are policy makers, and others are educators.

Parents who view themselves as actively engaged in education, and who take a participatory role in their child's education, rather than a passive one, are often the kind of parents who find their concern has caused them to seek home education as an alternative. They see their educator role as an integral part of their parental role. Dissatisfied with current educational options for their children, they become actively involved with this alternative.

REASONS FOR CHOOSING HOME SCHOOLING

Parental reasons vary for choosing this alternative. Social, academic, moral, psychological, and religious reasons are cited. Religious reasons are the prime motivation in the majority of the cases, but it is seldom mentioned as the *only* reason.

Parent-educators are an eclectic group. Each family has its own value system and its own reasons for home schooling. They cannot be lumped together in one category. The ideological reasons for "unschooling" by one family may differ drastically from the the academic reasons of another family, and may also differ from the religious reasons of yet another family. One parent may strive for more structure and higher academic achievement, while another may believe that the whole concept of structured learning is psychologically inhibiting to the child.

One woman explained her reasons as a paradox:

> **The schools were not teaching her children,**
> **AND**
> **The schools were teaching her children.**

The explanation is that the schools were not teaching her children academically, but were teaching a realm of moral and social values that conflicted with hers.

"Most do it because they think their children get a better education at home," explained Billie Jean Bryan of Georgia, adding, "In Georgia, the schools are not academically good."

Mrs. Bryan may be more accurate than she realizes. Academically, the Southeast has the largest proportion of elementary students in the lowest achievement group in studies done in 1971 and 1980. And only five states spent less than Georgia per capita on education in the school year 1979-1980.

The 1980 Gallup Poll of the Public's Attitude Toward the Public Schools showed a 10-year trend of lower ratings for public schools. In 1974, 18% of the people polled gave the schools an "A" rating, but by 1982 the percentage giving an "A" rating had dropped to only 8%. In the same time period, the percentage giving the schools a "C" rating had risen to 33% from 21%. The ratings were given to public schools in the participant's own community. When asked to rate public schools nationally, the ratings were even lower, and the more educated the participant, the lower his opinion of public schools.

The Gallup Poll shows that the American public regards the lack of discipline as the biggest problem in the public schools. Parents whose children are in public schools feel this way, as well as parents whose children are not in public schools. As Hillary Rodham Clinton noted in her 1996 book, *It Takes a Village*, there are 135,000 children who take guns to school every day. It's because of problems like this that homeschooling has become such a giant trend in the 1990s.

> **135,000 CHILDREN TAKE GUNS TO SCHOOL EVERY DAY**

Also criticized is the use of schools as a political and social tool. Since schools are financially supported by the government, many parents believe that certain viewpoints are biased. The government's monopoly on the school provides an excellent podium for propaganda.

Teachers' use of their captive audience to expound their political and moral theories bothers some parents. "Have you ever met a teacher who needed an invitation to tell you his opinion?" one parent asked.

Political, social, and moral opinions filter to the student from administrators, teachers, and other students. Parents see themselves as being responsible for shaping the types of exposures to which their children are subject, until the child is mature enough to defend his moral and social choices.

"We disagree with the social and moral values propagated in the schools," Cheryl Patricella said, citing examples of early dating and peer pressures. "And if your kid isn't *in*, the other kids will cut him into shreds for his entire life."

Religious fundamentalists want their children to receive adequate religious training in school. Although fundamentalist schools do exist, the locations of the schools may not be convenient for many parents. Likewise, the schools may not meet the state's requirements, thus some people have chosen home schooling as a means of meeting their religious objectives.

Professional educators are among the ranks of home schoolers, some for religious reasons. The Wagners of Washington state said: "We want to be the most influential people in our children's lives. Our main reason for keeping them at home is spiritual, but we are concerned with academic excellence. I want to provide the best for each child along the way."

Religious and moral issues are closely related. Sometimes the schools are teaching morals or ethics, which raises parental objections. "I don't want the schools to teach religion. But I was seeing things that clashed with what we were teaching the kids at home," Bette Norman said after she took her two daughters out of Minnesota schools. She subsequently placed them in a fundamentalist school, but found that the beliefs taught were different from their Catholic background. Finally, she and her husband decided to teach the girls at home using a religious-based home correspondence course offered by the Christian Liberty Academy.

Parents also have chosen this alternative to be able to spend more time with their children. Studies show the average school-age child spends only fourteen minutes a week talking with his parents. A 1989 Priority Management Systems report

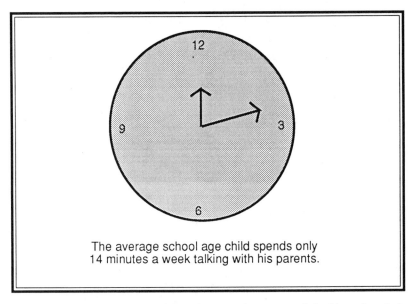

The average school age child spends only
14 minutes a week talking with his parents.

found that 53% of parents spend less than two hours a week looking after their children, and 42% of them do not read to their youngsters. Home schoolers are shocked by these statistics, and they are interested in keeping their family unit intact.

CONTROVERSIES

The issue of home schooling is definitely controversial. Legal, social, psychological, and educational aspects all have been debated by parents, educators and lawmakers.

Educators' attitude.

Although in the minority, there are some professional educators who are negative about parent-educators. Albert DeMartin, Jr., Superintendent of Schools in Hamilton, New Jersey, said that home schooling is a parent's right, but he added, "My

A recent encouraging note is the following letter from former President Reagan to Dr. Raymond Moore, that clearly states a former President's positions as pro-home schooling:

August 28, 1984

Dear Dr. Moore:

Thank you for your letter of July 6 informing me about the "renaissance of home education," and about your leadership in this movement.

As you know, I have on many occasions stated my belief that parents should have the widest possible choice in selecting an education for their children. It is encouraging to know that so many states are changing laws so that parents who choose home education may have that option.

Quality education and parental choice should never be conflicting goals, and I am delighted to see our country making progress in promoting both goals, whether in public schools, private schools, or home schools. I applaud those parents who care enough to be personally involved in the education of their children.

Thank you for what you are doing to encourage excellence in education and for taking the time to write.

Sincerely,

Ronald Reagan

Other members of the Reagan administration also established themselves as pro-choice. Gary Bauer of the United Stated Department of Education was in favor of a voucher system that would allow parents to use their tax money for the kind of education they choose for their children. Under that kind of system, the parents receive a voucher which they would use as cash to select the school of their choice—whether it be public, private or any other alternative. Unfortunately, this innovative idea has been virtually squashed by objections from the NEA (National Education Association), a teacher's labor union.

professional opinion is that it's a mistake. I don't know if any parent can provide through home education what schools are bound to provide through law."

Another critic, Nebraska educator James O'Hanlon said, "In the long run, the parent does the child a vast disservice."

However, the majority of educators are willing to look at each home schooling case before making a judgment. Ninety percent of the educators in my survey (Chapter 11) said that home schooling is sometimes beneficial to children, depending on the factors involved, and 93% said they would be willing to cooperate with home schoolers.

The general attitude of educators was expressed by Ronald Snyder of Pennsylvania, "A home education can only be as good as the parent makes it. A persistent, highly motivated parent with high expectations and a stimulating environment may be able to give their young children a quality education."

Legal.

All states and the District of Columbia allow some form of home schooling. Every state also has compulsory attendance laws of some sort. These laws vary from permissive to rigid. Some states are becoming more liberal, while others are becoming more strict, allowing only certified teachers to teach their own children following the most rigorous guidelines. Other states allow all parents freedom of choice in their children's education.

The vagueness of the law in some states has parents confused. The law might read that compulsory attendance requirements may be met by attendance in a private or parochial school, but might not define private or parochial school. Is a parent teaching a child at home a private school? In some states, home schoolers have applied for, and been granted, this status.

The lack of a universal thread, or even a universal trend, in home schooling laws is perplexing at best. Parents generally must be certain of exactly what their state compulsory attendance laws intend and find out how it applies to them.

The controversy starts when home schoolers are taken to court over their basic constitutional rights. The controversy continues when the legal issues move to certification or equivalency battles. These legal aspects are explored in Chapters 8-9.

Psychological.

A few critics have suggested that the child may be psychologically damaged by home schooling. One educator in my survey said one disadvantage is that the home-taught child might feel different from the other children in his neighborhood.

Another educator, James O'Hanlon, said he believes such a child would develop no further than his parents, and that his "ideas would be limited to the parent's notions of what is good and fit."

These critics make one wonder what happened in the case of the home schooled Abraham Lincoln. Did he just happen to develop beyond his parents, or was it that his parents just didn't become famous?

Studies of public education point to the vast permanent psychological damage that *schools* inflict on children. A 1989 report by the Carnegie Council on Adolescent Development, a program of the Carnegie Corporation, stated that the future for 7 million young people is in serious jeopardy because these teenagers are vulnerable to school failure, drug abuse, alcohol abuse, early sexual activity, and other dangerous activities. The organization blamed schools, stating that a "volatile mismatch exists between the organization and curriculum of middle grade schools and the intellectual and emotional needs of young adolescents." The report recommended far-reaching changes in the way that teenagers are treated during the middle grades, including smaller, more family-like school environments.

Home schools alleviate this problem by providing an atmosphere that is friendly to learning. Parents know that the emotional intensity involved in education is indicative that a secure relationship must exist before learning can take place. This bonding is overlooked in public education. Even psychologists point out that a child is more likely to emulate an adult who is warm and nurturing. These issues are further explored in Chapter 2.

HOME SCHOOLS: An Alternative

Social.

Social development in the home schooled child is mistakenly viewed by most educators as stagnant. They believe that the child needs school for his social needs, if not for the academic. Elly Rearick of Pennsylvania said: "I will be interested in the outcome of these children. Are they going to be able to adjust to society?"

This issue is probably the one that I personally feel most strongly about. Not only is the home schooled child's social development *not* stagnant but it is the *schools* that develop social stagnation. Schools stratify the young, beginning the first year, and the social stratification intensifies each year. By the time the children are in junior high, they have no idea how to socialize with anyone outside their peer group. The very idea of socializing with anyone not their own age is appalling to these children. They are unable to enter into the simplest conversation with adults or younger children. When they finally graduate from high school, and enter the society at large, they have to spend several years re-adjusting their attitudes until they fit. Some are never able to do this.

On the other hand, home schooled children learn to socialize with people of all ages. Their socialization takes place much more naturally than in the stilted environment of schools. They are much more able to disregard the strong peer pressure of the teen years and are more likely to be able to make their own decisions, regardless of what the crowd tells them. Home schooling creates individuals, not clones.

Home schoolers believe that using school as a tool for social interaction alone misses the point. Children can socialize after the academics at home as well as at school. It's the quality of the social interactions that matter, not the quantity.

The social issues are explored in detail in Chapter 3.

Religious.

Since traditionally most home schoolers in the United States have chosen this alternative primarily for religious reasons, their viewpoints have a direct bearing on how most people view home schooling. There seems to be a direct correlation between the phrase *secular humanism* and religious home schooling.

From my direct experiences with home schoolers and also with the media, I have found that there is a misunderstanding of the intentions of religious home schoolers and why they object to secular humanism in the schools. One radio interviewer went so far as to tell me he believed home schooling is a form of child abuse, and he immediately became angry when a caller mentioned *secular humanism*. This experience seeded my determination to find out more about religious home schoolers.

Later, I found that many other interviewers, as well as the public in general, did not understand what the term *secular humanism* means, and why home schoolers find it objectionable in schools. I felt that part of this book should attempt to help these groups understand each other. I wanted to paint a clearer picture so that there is less misunderstanding. Information about religious home schoolers is found in Chapter 4.

Academic.

Opponents of home schooling are quick to believe that parents cannot provide an adequate education for their children. They believe the lack of facilities and the lack of certified teachers will hinder children from learning.

Home schoolers point to the fact that Harvard, Yale, William & Mary, Antioch, Texas A & M, and Brigham Young University, among others, all have accepted home-educated students to their ranks. Scores on standardized tests generally are high for home schooled students, and students returning to public schools from a period of home schooling usually are ahead of grade level.

Academic issues are explored in Chapters 5 and 6.

Summary.

Even the most ardent home schooler admits that it's not for everyone.

HOME SCHOOLS: An Alternative

Parents choosing this alternative must commit time and energy to the task, and sometimes they even have had to defend their choices in court. In many families, both parents are working fulltime, and this type of schooling is obviously not for them. As one soft-spoken mother said, "I'm for home schools, but it's a personal matter."

HOMESCHOOLING MOVING TO THE NEW MILLENIUM

I've been involved with the homeschooling movement for over a decade now, and I've seen some changes. A very apparent change is that homeschooling is becoming more mainstream, and less radical. Homeschoolers are now respected and admired, whereas ten years ago they were simply a curiosity.

Another obvious change is that more people are choosing homeschooling as a reaction against the public schools, such as violence, poor student performance, and poor student attitudes in schools. Ten years ago, most homeschoolers chose this alternative for religious reasons, but today it's a growing trend for everyone. I recently had an exhibit booth at the Women's Expo in Phoenix, Arizona, which was attended by more than 50,000 women. This show gave me tremendous feedback to what women are thinking. Of the women who came by with preschool children, at least half of them indicated that they *absolutely will not put their precious children* in public schools. Think of that, half of them are considering homeschooling or other alternatives. If that trend continues, homeschooling will prove to be the most major trend in modern education ever!

This growing trend in education is a many-faceted issue. Whatever the controversies may be, the fact remains that this trend is growing rapidly and becoming more appealing to a larger segment of Americans.

Parents once again have found that they truly can educate their children, that they can develop study schedules, that they can choose a curriculum, and that they and their children can be richly rewarded emotionally by the task.

CHAPTER TWO
The Psychological and Emotional Aspects

Ask a friend to tell you a joke about school. Then ask another friend to tell a school joke. Then ask another friend to tell a school joke. The jokes you hear may be similar to these:

1.
Teacher: Jim, please define "ignorance."
Jim: Ignorance is when you don't know something, and the teacher finds out.

2.
Teacher: Willie, can you tell me what a hypocrite is?
Willie: It's a boy who comes to school with a smile on his face.

3.
Teacher: Jonah, what are you doing—learning something?
Jonah: No, I'm listening to you.

4.
Teacher: This exam will be conducted on the honor system. Now take seats three apart and every other row.

The content of jokes reflects people's attitudes toward a subject. Pick up a joke book and read all the jokes about schools and teachers. What do they have in common?

Negativity. Even in jest, people talk about how much they dislike school and how it causes them anxiety and fear. The first joke above shows an example of "strategies," how children strive to find ways just to get through school, but when someone else finds out, the game is up.

The second joke is easy to analyze: Kids hate school. Adults and children alike take this hatred for granted.

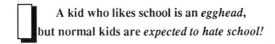

A kid who likes school is an *egghead*, but normal kids are *expected to hate school!*

The third joke tells about a situation we all know—while the children must sit quietly and behave, the teacher can rattle on endlessly about any subject that interests him.

The fourth joke reflects the general attitude of teachers and schools: that children are inherently untrustworthy. Those values are not the kind that parents want their children learning.

Dreams are also an indicator of a person's emotions. Some feelings expressed in one's dreams are those that might have been repressed at one time; others are feelings that still linger. Dreams about fearful school experiences are common among children and adults. One adult related this school dream:

> *My recurring school dream was that I had enrolled in some course and then completely forgotten about it. So that when exam time and grade time came, I was in total terror, knowing I'd fail and it was too late to do anything about it. I can feel the fear now, and it's 20 plus years later.*

Adults and children alike tell about frightening dreams they have had about school. They describe feelings of rushing through halls to find a class and not being able to find it; of frantically running to the girl's restroom to hide from a cruel teacher or student; of feeling panic when the bell rang when they were a block away from school; and of being laughed at for giving the wrong answer in class. Dreams vividly reflect people's real feelings about school: **FEAR**.

FEAR, PRESSURE, TENSION

Patrick was a happy 5-year-old, always singing and playing games with his family. Of all the children in his family, he was the one who most often could be heard singing. Finding Patrick during the day was easy. His mother simply listened for echoes of "Ol' MacDonald's Farm" or "Three Blind Mice." In fact, he sang day and night, not stopping until the sandman threw sleep dust his way.

Singing was only one way that Patrick expressed his zest for life. He also enjoyed playing games with his family. Even with his older brothers, Patrick showed that he could be a competent softball player. When his older sisters played jump rope, he could chant with them:

> *Cinderella dressed in yellow*
> *Went upstairs to kiss a fellow.*
> *By mistake, she kissed a snake.*
> *How many doctors did it take?*
> *1,2,3,4,5 ...*

Mom and Dad were pleased that he could recite his ABC's and already knew the basics of adding and subtracting. They were proud of their little man as they sent him off to kindergarten.

Within a few short weeks of the beginning of school, the family noticed a drastic change within Patrick: He stopped singing.

He also stopped playing with his brothers and sisters. When the rest of the family went to play, Patrick withdrew to his room. He ignored invitations to join the games. He became sullen and quiet.

Danielle lived far away from Patrick but went to a school very similar to his. She was seven and had adjusted to going to school. At least apparently she had. But each day when it was time to go to school, she developed a "tummy ache." Her mother tried to persuade her that the pain would go away as soon as she saw her friend at school, but to no avail.

HOME SCHOOLS: An Alternative

Sending Danielle to school became a battle every day. The tears, the apparent anguish, and the pleading were traumatic to Danielle and her family.

Thousands of parents testify that their school-age children exhibit symptoms similar to those of Patrick and Danielle, reactions to the stress of School. Just look at the list of school-related tension-releasing habits compiled by a child development expert:

Stuttering　　　　　　　　　　　*Nail-biting*
Thumb-sucking　　　　　　　　　*Hand-to-mouth gestures*
Sticking tongue out　　　　　　　*Twisting mouth*
Biting lips　　　　　　　　　　　*Chewing pencil*
Clearing throat　　　　　　　　　*Throaty noises*
Shaking legs　　　　　　　　　　*Knocking knees*
Throwing small items　　　　　　*Shifting eyes*
Playing with teeth　　　　　　　*Rolling eyes*
Dropping pencils　　　　　　　　*Laying head on arms*
Grimacing　　　　　　　　　　　*Scowling*
Raising eyebrows　　　　　　　　*Fiddling with chairs*
Sighing　　　　　　　　　　　　*Blowing through lips*
Plucking eyelids

Parents add the following to the list:

Tummy aches　　　　　　　　　*Crying spells*
Tantrums　　　　　　　　　　　*Irritability*
Sleeplessness　　　　　　　　　*Personality changes*
Slapping　　　　　　　　　　　*Withdrawal*
Excitability　　　　　　　　　　*Confusion*
Whimpering
Excessive fighting with siblings

And on and on until the list sounds like a bad dream. To say that entering school can be traumatic is a bit of an understatement. Early school years are a source of many irritating nervous habits, some of which continue through life.

Fear is an inherent part of the structure of school, from the beginning of kindergarten. Remember being 5 years old? The first day of school a very small child enters a very big world. The school looks enormous to him. The person in charge is also very large. Teacher takes charge, and immediately the child understands where the control is—in this big, big person.

The child, already fearful of separation from his parents, is thrust into a cold situation. However caring the teacher may want to be, there is no time in the day for intimate contact with each of the students. Therefore, the child moves from his very loving world at home to an impersonal businesslike atmosphere.

The next thing he learns at school is that there are many rules limiting his behavior. He may not speak unless allowed. He may not move until ordered. And he may not associate with his peers until told. All of these rules are enforced through an element of fear. As John Holt says in *How Children Fail*::

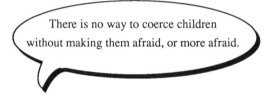

There is no way to coerce children without making them afraid, or more afraid.

Psychologists have a name for this fear: *school phobia*. It can strike children from kindergarten through college and may plague them the rest of their lives. Dr. John C. Collidge, senior psychologist at the Judge Baker Guidance Center, found that children with school phobia often run into psychological problems later in life.

Thus fear is the first indoctrination of the child into a cycle of negativity. As school continues, he learns more negativity. Other children also are afraid of school, but they all must learn to produce to please the teacher. Children are normally very productive on their own, but when forced to produce in specific ways they become disenchanted with learning.

The pressure is on. The child knows that he is expected to follow the teacher's plans for learning. He must have the right answers at the right time. If he doesn't, he will be censured by the teacher and possibly ridiculed by the other students. His peers, fearful of their own shortcomings, develop an attitude of: "I'm afraid that if I give the wrong answer, the teacher will make them laugh at me, so if Peter says something wrong, I'm going to laugh. Then maybe Peter will be afraid to laugh at me."

One fear leads to another. From the fear of making a mistake grows the fear of trying. The cycle continues.

LOSS OF IDENTITY, STEREOTYPING, CLONES

School teaches a child that *specific answers are good* and that anything else is *bad*. A question may not be answered with a question, and only teachers may ask questions. The answer to "Who discovered America?" is not designed to open a discussion period. Even though the *right answer* to that question is debatable, the student better be ready to give a stock answer.

Not being able to design any type of approach to a subject leads children to a loss of identity. They are no longer individuals, they are part of a *class*.

Students lose identity at the very time when they should be shaping it. At the very crucial period of their lives when they should be learning how to make decisions, they are not allowed to make any. The very tools they need to make sense of the world, to feel self-worth, and to enhance their own dignity, are denied to them. The result is self-loss instead of self-gain.

The loss of identity comes not only from the structure of the standard classroom, but also from the grading system. Designed to classify students, it robs them of their individuality. He is not John, he is an "A" student. She is not Marta, she is a "C" student. He is not Philip, he is a "Level 1, Underachiever."

Stereotyping of students begins early. Grades are given in early elementary school. Once graded, always graded. The entrapping system never lets loose of its victims. Once a "C" student, always a "C" student. Even changing schools doesn't change the stigma because the grades are always essential for transferring. Teachers always review the previous grades of a transfer student. Doomed to mediocrity for life.

The label sticks with the child forever. One teacher passes on to the next a certain number of A's, B's, C's, D's, and F's.

HOME SCHOOLS: An Alternative

> They might as well be stamped on the forehead like graded cattle, because the label will follow them all the way through school.

Studies have shown that teachers' expectations of students actually may determine the students' performance. It's called the self-fulfilling prophecy. If Peter constantly treats his son, David, like an imbecile, eventually David will act like one. If a teacher is told that her group of pupils is gifted, she will treat them like intelligent people, and very likely they will respond as such, even if they are actually a normal mixture of talents.

Unfortunately, the negative aspect of the self-fulfilling prophecy usually is seen in schools. Teachers pass on negative labels of students indiscriminately, and these practices create boxes that trap children forever. An attorney for a North Carolina home schooling family said of schools, "We're getting to the point where everybody has to run through a little mill and where individuality is allowed less and less."

Schools turn out a very un-individual, a clone, a robot. The cycle continues.

LOSS OF CREATIVITY, LOSS OF INITIATIVE

Through fear, the child loses his identity. Through his loss of identity, he loses his creativity. He is afraid to try anything new, to examine the world on his own. There is no initiative left. School has led him to believe that he must be *taught* in order to *learn* and that there is no learning without specified answers. For him, learning is something given, not taken.

> *Modern education too often covers the fingers with rings, and at the same time cuts the sinews at the wrist.*
> **John Sterling, 1806-1844**
> **British Essayist**

Chapter Two: The Psychological & Emotional Aspect

HOME SCHOOLS: An Alternative

Children are fed volumes of "facts" by a system that proceeds to choke off their talents. What the child really learns in this entire process is how to avoid true learning while appearing to be busy, how to look industrious while the teacher is looking, how to sneak a note to his friend while the teacher's back is turned, and how to turn in mediocre work just to get by.

Stanley Thompson Jr., a sophomore at Los Angeles High School, wrote an editorial for the *Los Angeles Times* in which he said: "Why are there very few students who treasure learning? Partly because American society projects the idea to young people that it is fine to be mediocre ... There is no motivation to strive for excellence ... Even worse, there is a feeling that being in the pursuit of excellence is not normal, and those who engage in that pursuit are not normal. This attitude tells young people that they will not be socially accepted if they seek knowledge."

SCHOOLS BREED MEDIOCRITY

The whole system seems to say to children: "It's OK to be mediocre, because once you're out in the 'real world,' that's all you need to give. Anyone who does more than the required minimum is a fool. In the working world, you nap anytime the boss isn't looking, and you only need to do what you were hired to do."

The result is a mass of humanity that is prepared to do no more than that, millions of followers with few leaders.

THE CYCLE OF NEGATIVITY

The cycle of negativity produced by schools is psychologically detrimental to a child. First fear puts him in his place. Then fear leads him to a loss of identity, and finally to a loss of creativity. Then it happens all over again because the child's loss of creativity leaves him blank and fearful.

An American educator, William P. Faunce, noted early in this century that the public schools had a great flaw:

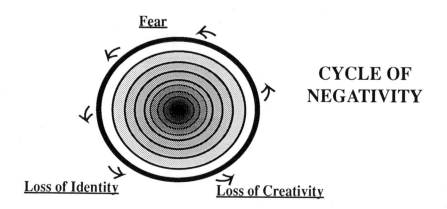

Fear

CYCLE OF NEGATIVITY

Loss of Identity

Loss of Creativity

> *We have in America the largest public school system on earth, the most expensive college buildings, the most extensive curriculum, but nowhere else is education so blind to its objectives, so indifferent to any specific outcome as in America. One trouble has been its negative character. It has aimed at suppression of faults rather than the creation of virtues.*

According to one study cited in Borg Hendrickson's book *Home School: Taking the First Step*, public school children lose their sense of self-worth dramatically as they progress through the grades, from 80% with a strong sense of self-worth when they begin public school, dropping to only 20% for fifth graders, and way down to 5% by the time they graduate from high school. What proof that public schools damage children!

HOW HOME SCHOOLING CAN HELP

Home schools can break the cycle of negativity. Even if a child has begun school and started the cycle, a change to education at home can help. Remember Patrick and Danielle at the beginning of the chapter? They are real little people who had big emotional problems because of school. Well, Patrick and Danielle were lucky. Their parents had the foresight to remove them from school and to begin teaching them at home. Patrick began singing again and Danielle's stomach pains disappeared.

Parents have pulled their children from public schools for a variety of reasons, but almost every one of them commented on the damaging psychological effects that schools have had on young people. Even if the parents' main rationale for home schooling was religious, ideological, or academic, they also mentioned the problems of the negative effect of schools upon children's individuality and creativity.

Parents who have never sent their children to public schools can ensure them of the strong emotional bond that is vital to their growth and development. These children can avoid the painful early separation that is so emotionally damaging to them.

The strong emotional bond between parent and child is more important to the child than most adults imagine. Strong parental love is crucial to the emotional, social, and cognitive (learning) development of the child. That tie not only provides love and security, but also provides the soil in which learning and adjustment to the outside world can take root.

A child learns about the world only after he feels secure about his place at home. Security prompts him to explore, to experiment, and to learn. The same feeling of security that leads him to interact with other people will help him learn about the world in which he lives.

Children in home schools have a better chance to develop their own identity. One mother home schooled the youngest three of her 10 children, and found striking differences between them and her publicly-schooled children:

> My children [who went to public school] had
> poor images of what they could do when they
> were growing up. These three [home
> schooled] have more security than the other
> ones who were in the [public school] system
> from the beginning.

HOME SCHOOLS: An Alternative

Even if a child has spent some years in public schools, a change to a home school can break the cycle of negativity. Released from all the bad feelings about school, the children regain their natural style of learning eagerly and enthusiastically.

Home schools provide a natural and loving environment for learning.

There is no use of fear in the home school, so the child will not develop negative feelings about learning. He will be positive about himself and will be able to think and act creatively.

Emotion is inseparable from the learning process and the success of that learning process depends on the kinds of emotions that develop between a teacher and the student. That's why home schools are better places emotionally for learning. The emotions shown at home are warm and secure.

Another plus for home education is flexibility, the lack of rigid schedules and curriculum. The majority of professional educators (62%, see Chapter 11), agree that home schools have the advantage of flexibility to allow the child to develop his interests, talents, and hobbies. The autonomous nature of the home school snaps the cycle of fear and uniformity found in schools.

Darrin Geisy of Virginia is a fine example of a young man whose home schooling helped free him from the cycle of negativity found in public schools. He attended public school for many years, but his last six years were spent learning at home. As a result, he developed interests and talents that might otherwise have been untried had he still been in public schools.

His most exciting project was the chance to play Charles Washington, brother of the President, in the miniseries *George Washington*. While working on a set at a dinner theater, Darrin was spotted by production people and offered the part.

Does Darrin believe that being home schooled had any influence in landing an acting role in the miniseries? Yes, because it allowed him the flexibility in his schedule that led to the job, plus the self-confidence to do it. In a home school

HOME SCHOOLS: An Alternative

environment, he said: "There isn't any negative attitudes, like in school, where kids get the feeling that you can't do things before you even try."

The use of rewards is an important psychological reinforcement used to promote learning (more in Chapter 6). Children love a special prize, even a gold star or a compliment from their teacher. Timing is crucial for the effectiveness of these rewards. For children, the immediacy of feedback is essential.

Home schools provide this immediate feedback system that is logistically impossible in public schools. The value of these rewards is enforced by the emotional bond between the parent and child, and provides another reason why this kind of schooling is so effective.

Proponents of home schools believe they will help provide the future's leaders: men and women with high self-esteem and with positive attitudes about their creative energies. Proof of this claim lies in the fact that many of the world's greatest talents have been home schooled, among them: George Washington, Franklin D. Roosevelt, Albert Einstein, and Winston Churchill.

HOME SCHOOLS BENEFIT PARENTS TOO!

The psychological benefits of home schools are two-fold: for the children *and* for the parents. Home schooling is very rewarding for parents. They are able to spend more time with their children and are able to see their children's creativity blossom.

A Pennsylvania mother explained how her experience was beneficial:

> *Home schooling has not only educated me (dinosaurs, mushrooms, etc); but as home schooling forces me to spend time with my children, it creates a closer relationship between us. I must be in tune with my children to know if they are ready for the next concept or if they will be frustrated and learn to hate not only the concept but the subject (example: math). The time together allows me greater understanding of my child which gives me more patience to deal with the problems of parenting.*

Chapter Two: The Psychological & Emotional Aspects | 35

HOME SCHOOLS: An Alternative

The best hours of the day rightly belong to those you love, home schoolers explain. When a child goes to public school, the teachers gets those hours, and parents get what's left over—usually a tired child. Home schooler Jennifer Lastine of Minnesota said, "I wouldn't give up the time I've spent with the children."

The benefits that parents have mentioned include: better family life due to the quality and quantity of time spent together; the chance to learn better parenting skills; increased patience; and the learning adventures encountered together. Some parents have discovered that learning need not be painful, an attitude that they had carried with them since their own school days.

One parent summed it up:

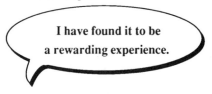

I have found it to be
a rewarding experience.

For more information about the concepts discussed in this chapter, check the following psychology studies:

The Child From Five to Ten, Arnold Gesell with Louis Bates and Francis Ilg, (revised edition), NY: Harper & Row, 1977.

Psychology of Adolescence: Behavior and Development, John Harrocks, Boston: Houghton-Mifflin, 1969.

Toward a Psychology of Being, Abraham Maslow (second edition), Princeton, NJ: Van Nostrand, 1968.

Pygmalion in the Classroom: Teacher Expectation and Pupils' Intellectual Development, David Rosenthal & Lenore Jacobson, NY: Holt, Rinehart & Winston, 1968. This book describes the phenomenon known to psychologists as the self-fulfilling prophecy, where a person will meet the personality and intellectual traits that another person treats him as possessing. The book describes a specific study where teachers were given false information concerning their pupils and thereafter treated the pupils in a manner which reflected this false information. If the information said that this particular group of students was gifted, the teachers treated the group as gifted, and the students responded by achieving as though they truly were gifted, even if indeed the group had really been found to be a normal mixture of intelligence.

CHAPTER THREE:
Social Aspects

One of the most frequent criticisms of home schools by people who have preconceived notions about the subject is that they believe that these children are missing out socially. More than 80% of the educators I surveyed believed that home schools were at a disadvantage in the social development of the child, and 59% believed that a disadvantage of home schools was the lack of competition in the child's academic and social world.

Educators were vehement in the support of public schools as a social tool. One teacher stated:

> *A child at home is isolated. It [home schooling] might seem fine now, but what will happen when these kids get out into the real world and Mom's not there any more?*
> *It's almost like putting up a glass house and saying nothing bad will ever happen.*
> *She [the home schooled child] is going to miss the interaction with other students. I don't know how to say this diplomatically, but I do not think that home schooling is appropriate for any children. It's a serious responsibility that the parent must recognize.*

The teachers and administrators who dislike the home school alternative would like parents to believe that these children will be socially stagnated or social misfits. In fact, some educators believe that parents who choose this kind of education must be social misfits themselves. For some reason, the very act of choosing to educate their own children sets parents up as radicals, when in fact they are choosing to do it for very logical and rational reasons.

Sometimes friends, neighbors, and relatives are also critical about a family's decision to home school. They may be afraid the children will not get along with other children. Their comments range from "Jonathan will become too dependent on his parents" to "Maureen will be left out of all of the fun."

These critics seem to believe the only way for children to learn social skills is at school, and that the family environment is lacking in this fundamental area.

"I don't agree with educators on that aspect," said one home schooler. And evidence from parents, child psychologists, and even from the children themselves all substantiates the claims of home schoolers that their children are not becoming socially inept. Quite the contrary—evidence points to the opposite. Children educated at home seem to have far greater social confidence than their public school peers.

HOW CHILDREN VIEW SOCIAL LIFE IN SCHOOL

In a school situation, children are constantly around their peers. They have no choice. Does this mean that they prefer to always be around children their own age? Does this mean that they can associate only with that group? Is the social life in school pleasant? How many adults remember what it was really like?

Most adults, if they try, can remember situations in which a fellow classmate was teased relentlessly for his accent, dress, physical appearance, social class, race, religion, or because they were new in school. Sometimes the teasing went too far, and the results were world-shattering for the child.

A college friend told me this story:

> *I remember a couple of years in junior high when my friends and I formed a club for the sole purpose to taunt and humiliate another girl in our class. We were all better-than-average students, including the victim.*

There seemed no apparent reason for our group's ringleader to isolate this one particular girl. She seemed identical to us in every respect. The cruelty we inflicted upon her was unbelievable. Besides being excluded from our group, she was jeered at, whispered about, and teased. We spent all of our free time thinking of ways to make her feel bad, trying to find horrid nicknames to call her, making up nasty songs about her, and convincing other people to chastise her.

If any one of us tried to defend the victim, which we occasionally did, we were instantly tormented by our leader, and that ended any further humane discussion.

The pain we must have caused that girl is embarrassing to think about now. She was pretty and talented, but the way we treated her definitely affected her the rest of the way through high school.

I've tried to analyze why our leader chose her to be our scapegoat, and why we followed her so meekly and for so long. Possibly our leader was jealous of this girl's close relationship with her mother, but I'm not sure. The reason the rest of the gang was so meek was probably due to our submissive behavior that had been drilled into us through school's rigid schedules and intolerant attitudes, but we were too young to be aware of it. I know that the way we treated her was not from a lack of ethics, but more from the impact that peer pressure had on us. School was definitely responsible in part for the way we viewed each other.

Through a child's eyes, school is not necessarily a friendly social environment. Every child could tell you that. Actually it's a competitive and mean place, where the pressure is on the children to conform to the way that the group sees fit. And usually the group is led by the most aggressive child, not by the child who has the best social skills.

You guessed it. The bully is in charge. For boys, proving themselves is a constant problem. Playground brawls and after-school fights plague them. The choices are either to stand up to the bully or to submit. Neither solution is as simple as it sounds.

If a boy chooses to resist harassment, he will probably have to fight. Winning means proving himself over and over again to each new bully that comes along to challenge him. If he chooses to give in, that means continual taunting, theft of lunch money, and other types of punishment.

A government study reports that hundreds of secondary school students are attacked *each month,* and that several million have something stolen in that same month. The same study found that one in four elementary students are afraid that somebody [another student] might hurt them at school.

The problem is so bad that a dozen researchers met at Harvard in 1987 during a two-day "Schoolyard Bully Practicum" to draft a national battle plan against schoolyard bullies, who conduct "peer terrorism." According to research brought up during the conference, these bullies are more likely to become adult criminals than their classmates. These experts also said that bullying contributes to teenage suicide, high school dropouts, and other problems. "I don't think most parents have any understanding of the problem," said Ronald Stephens, director of the National School Safety Center in Encino, California.

**This is the type of socialization that educators
are worried about home schoolers missing?**

This type of social environment in the schools is typical, not just in lower class neighborhoods, but in suburbia and rural towns as well. Kids with money aren't immune to peer problems. As children approach adolescence, the pressure to conform is even greater.

HOW PARENTS VIEW SOCIAL LIFE IN SCHOOL

When asked about their views concerning social values developed in schools, parents react intensely. They cite problems of drug use, violence, aberrant

HOME SCHOOLS: An Alternative

behavior, sexual promiscuity, smoking, vulgar language, and poor attitudes. They attribute most of this conduct to the acute peer pressure experienced in schools.

Dr. Gustavsen's study showed that 86% of home schoolers believe that there is too much rivalry and ridicule in schools and that 93% of them believe that there is too much violence in schools.

The public ranked number 3 the use of drugs as a major problem in public schools in a recent Gallup poll. *NBC Nightly News*, September 20, 1989, reported a recent survey showed 78% of parents said there were drugs in their child's school. In recent years, students have held other students hostage at gunpoint. It happened in a suburban Phoenix high school in 1988, and in Kentucky in 1989. Bomb threats [often by irate or emotionally disturbed students] have happened in the most unlikely of schools, and are a common problem.

Of the educators I surveyed, 62% were aware that one of the reasons parents choose home schooling is because of the drugs, violence, and other social problems in the schools.

Children learn much misbehavior in school. Parents are upset that they spend so much time teaching their children good values, but their children come home from school using totally unacceptable language, becoming aggressive with each other, and being pressured by friends to smoke or use drugs. No matter how strong the family value system might be, the hours children spend with their peers erode away those values and replace them with inferior ones.

In 1940, teachers were asked to rate their worst problems with students, which at the time were:

1....Talking
2....Chewing gum
3....Making noise
4....Running in the halls
5....Getting out of turn in line
6....Not putting paper in wastebaskets

Yes, one of their biggest problems in 1940 was to get kids to put waste paper in the trash can! Compare that to teachers' worst problems with students in 1980:

1....Rape	9....Vandalism
2....Robbery	10...Extortion
3....Assault	11...Drug abuse
4....Burglary	12...Alcohol abuse
5....Arson	13...Gang warfare
6....Bombings	14...Pregnancies
7....Murder	15...Abortions
8....Suicide	16...Venereal disease

WHAT ABOUT PUBLIC EDUCATION IN THE 1990S?

A California teacher explained what education in the 1990s means, "A lot of what the teachers in my building do is just try to keep the students in line. Teaching is secondary." As we noted before, Hillary Rodham Clinton's book, *It Takes a Village*, states that 135,000 children take guns to school *every day*!

U.S. News and World Report, November 8, 1993, reported that, "Today, more than three million crimes are year are committed in or near the 85,000 U.S. public schools."

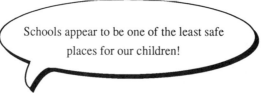

Schools appear to be one of the least safe places for our children!

A+ FOR HOME SCHOOL SOCIAL LIFE

Right about now, I can imagine the thoughts of the reader. You're saying, "We know about the problems of peer pressure, but won't home schooled children go through the same thing? Why would home schooling be any better?"

The Family Circus
Bil Keane

HOME SCHOOLS: An Alternative

Parents who have chosen home schooling have emphatically said, "Home schooling is good for the social development of children! It helps the child to develop the strength to say 'NO' to peer pressure."

I asked each parent I interviewed, "What is your view on your child's social development?" Every one of them had an absolutely glowing report on how education at home had a positive social influence on their children.

Bette Norman of Minnesota reported that her children became more socially confident after they were removed from school because, "Children in schools try to adapt to suit the group. At home they can develop their own personality."

A South Dakota woman remarked, "Society has tabooed kids who are not with kids their own age. My children may be home schooled, but they are not isolated. They get alone fine socially. In fact, they have a well-balanced ability to socialize with all ages."

Home schooled children can actually have a much better social development than their publicly schooled peers because they are more likely to learn how to communicate with adults and children of all ages instead of just one isolated category. Home provides a natural environment for social growth versus school's stilted environment.

"School is not meant to be a social place," said Barbara Boone, a Colorado private school teacher. And indeed, it is not. The child attends school, but has only superficial contact with other students and the teacher. That shallow interaction is the problem with school's rigid environment. True social skills cannot be developed that way. The mere presence of other people is not enough. The quality of social interaction matters the most.

What types of social activities do home schooled children engage in? Church-related activities, community groups, Girl Scouts, Boy Scouts, and 4-H are high on their list. Unlike schools, community groups do not deny their activities to children just because they are home schooled. The types of activities chosen have a high correlation to the types of values that parents wish their children to develop, and also provide the types of activities children need in order to develop their own unique talents and interests, such as music and drama groups. Home schooled children tend to join groups for the involvement in special projects, not just because "all of my friends are doing it."

These parents seem to prefer non-competitive sports, such as hiking, canoeing, spelunking, and swimming, although a few do encourage their sons to join Little League baseball.

An interesting observation about home schooling parents is that they are not social misfits, as some educators would like to believe. They fit into the mainstream socially. They are typically neither too aggressive nor too passive.

There was a study done by the University of Michigan, Ann Arbor, Michigan. This study found that children educated at home don't become social misfits. In fact, it found that more than three-quarters of them believed that homeschooling had helped them interact with people from different levels of society. The entire article appears in the *Home Education Resource Guide*, available from Blue Bird Publishing.

Another hypothesis of educators is that home schooled children do not get along with teachers or other children, so their parents remove them from school. Gustavsen's study showed that 92% of these children do get along with teachers, and that 90% of them get along with other children.

Parents do not remove their children from school to run away from social development, but rather to improve the type of social development that their children have. Jackie Sipe of Tucson, Arizona, a former third grade teacher, and a current home schooler, said that she isn't worried about the social development of her daughter because, "I can monitor her social behavior much better."

One of the criticisms of home schools is that people believe these children won't have enough time to be around other kids so that they can learn how to be a kid. However, it's not important to teach a kid how to be a kid. They already know that. It's important to teach a kid how to be a good person. That's the purpose of social interaction.

Parents are always excusing erratic behavior in their children by saying, "Oh, he's just being a kid." Then all of a sudden when the child reaches a certain age, the parents start asking him, "Why don't you grow up?" Wouldn't it be better to teach him all along how to act in a reasonable manner? Social development is helped by being treated like a decent, responsible person, even when that person is still very young.

That's the main reason why social development of home schooled children is so natural. They aren't shoved into a room with 25 other kids their age and told not to speak, not to move, not to do anything except when told. They are interacting socially all day long in a very natural manner. They are being treated like rational human beings and being shown how to be a responsible person without having their rights taken away.

> **HOME SCHOOLS PROVIDE NATURAL
> AND LOVING SOCIAL RELATIONSHIPS!**

EXPERTS ON SOCIAL DEVELOPMENT

Parents approve of home schooling for social development and children benefit from it. Still, a few skeptics might want to say: "That wouldn't work. All the experts say so." Just for these skeptics, this section has been included to examine what child development experts say about social development. A list of books for additional reading is at the end of the chapter.

What is social development? It is the learning of skills for interaction with people. Specific skills are:

✓Forming personal attachments—learning to like other people and having them like you.

✓Expression—learning how to communicate, not just about the physical world, but about feelings.

✓Self control.

✓Knowledge of types of dispositions and personalities—knowing the difference between Grumpy, Sleepy, and Happy.

✓Knowledge of different types of social situations—how to act in a church, how to act at a party, how to act in a restaurant, how to act in a store.

✓Knowledge of different types of social interactions—how to introduce yourself to someone, what to do if you're embarrassed, not to stare at people in public.

✓Knowledge of different types of social relationships—the difference between a mother-child relationship and a storekeeper-child relationship.

✓Learning social roles—how to be a parent, how to be a friend.

How do children learn these skills? Through problem-solving, cooperation, helping, participating, and watching.

The child's first social relationship is obviously with his parents. Through imitating his parents, he learns how to act. When his parents reward or punish him for his actions, he learns whether or not the action was good. As the child grows, he also interacts with other children. His peers help him gain more knowledge about social relationships.

How important are the parents to the child's social development? Absolutely crucial, because they are the most important people in his life. Through imitating them, he will learn social patterns that will be used the rest of his life.

When a child enters school at the tender age of 5, he has a new adult influence in his life. This will complicate his life. One developmental expert, Arnold Gesell, said,

> In fact the child from 5 to 10 is at the apex of a triangle of interpersonal forces. Life would apparently be much easier for him if he had to adjust only to his parents or only to his teachers.

Another expert cites the danger of early separation of children from parents. Dr. Raymond Moore notes that a child's self concept is learned through attachments to the parent, and this self image must be solidly formed before the child can effectively learn to socialize with other people. When we send a child to school so young, it's no wonder that he becomes an appendage of the school. He has not yet learned to be himself.

Peer group orientation begins too early for school children, and is a definite disadvantage. It will wean children away from the parents at too young an age and cause unnecessary tensions between them, especially at a time when the children still need their parents so much. It will also propel children into viewpoints and actions that are antisocial rather than social.

One widely accepted theory is called the social learning theory. It means that people learn behavior from watching other people. Children imitate the behavior of people they admire or identify with.

Albert Bandura conducted research on this theory. Different groups of children were shown films of adults acting in aggressive ways, or live adults acting aggressively, or cartoons of people acting aggressively. A control group was not shown anything. Each group of children was then watched for 20 minutes of free play, and the number of times these children acted in an aggressive manner was compared.

The children who had watched someone act aggressively, either in person or in film or in cartoons, had twice as many acts of aggression during the time period as those in the control group, who did not see anyone act aggressively.

The conclusion is obvious that children learn by watching other people's actions, and younger children cannot distinguish for themselves which acts are appropriate to imitate and which are not. That's why they need their parents until they are old enough to make these value judgments for themselves.

The social learning theory is of particular interest to home schoolers. These parents wish to be the most important people in their children's lives. They wish to be the role models for their children to learn values. However, kids in schools are learning values and behavior from strangers. That's why normally well-behaved kids come home from school and act in ways that their parents do not approve.

Spending too much time with peers also makes children peer-dependent. If a child has not yet developed his self identity, the child can begin to feel worthless as an individual and lose respect for his parents. He turns heavily to peer influence at this point. If he is rejected by his peers, he may not be able to weather it emotionally. He could end up feeling incompetent for the rest of his life.

The teen years are especially vulnerable to peer pressure. The teenager is going through a period where identity development is crucial, and he cannot develop individuality if he is peer dependent. Decisions about smoking, drugs, and sexual behavior will be decided by the group, not the individual.

Home schoolers realize the problems of peer pressure, but they have not thrown in the towel in despair. Instead, they realize that a close family bond will overcome these problems, and that is why they have chosen this alternative education for their kids.

Thus, when educators criticize home schools for lack of social development, parents point proudly to their children's social successes, and can defend themselves with studies from child development experts themselves.

The home is the best place to begin developing social skills, not just for the first four years, but for all of the childhood years. As one parent put it, "You're talking about how a child learns to act. If he is taught to be kind, to share, to be polite, that's how he will act when he goes out into society."

THESE BOOKS CAN TELL YOU MORE ABOUT SOCIAL DEVELOPMENT:

"Imitation of film-mediated aggressive models," an article by Albert Bandura, Dorothea M. Ross and Sheila A. Ross. Published in the *Journal of Abnormal and Social Psychology,* 1963: Volume 66, pages 3-11. This article describes the study in which children were shown aggressive models and imitated their behavior.

Social Learning Theory Albert Bandura, Englewood Cliffs, NJ: Prentice-Hall, 1977.

The Developing Person, Kathleen Stassen Berger, NY: Worth Publishers, 1980.

Children & Adolescents: Interpretive Essays on Jean Piaget , David Elkind, NY: Oxford University Press, 1974. This book explains the theories of Jean Piaget, one of the most studied child development writers of all time.

Jean Piaget: the Man and His Ideas , Richard I. Evans, NY: EP Dutton & Co., 1973.

The Child From Five to Ten , (revised edition) Arnold Gesell with Louis Bates and Frances Ilg, NY: Harper & Row, 1977.

Better Late Than Early , Dr. Raymond & Dorothy Moore, NY: Reader's Digest Press, 1975.

School Can Wait , Dr. Raymond & Dorothy Moore, Provo UT: Brigham University Press, 1979.

Science and Human Behavior, B.F.Skinner, NY: Macmillan, 1953. Mr. Skinner is a reknown child development expert.

Beyond Freedom and Dignity, B.F. Skinner, NY: Knopf, 1971.

CHAPTER FOUR:
Religious and Moral Issues

R eligion has traditionally been the most commonly cited reason for parents to choose home schooling. They feel that the moral training of their children is their responsibility, not the state's.

Gustavsen's study found that the number one reason for home schools was that parents believe public schools are a threat to the moral health of their children. The second strongest reason was that the parents felt public schools do not aid in desirable character development.

Findings by support groups across the country verify these results. The leader of a Michigan organization found in the 1980s that 75% of the parents in his home school group chose that alternative for religious reasons. In Missouri, another group's leader stated:

> *Almost all of the people we have helped start [home schools] are devout Christians who will not allow any earthly authority to approve a school [meaning their home school] that has been founded on Christian conviction. How can a lower authority approve a higher authority?*

Home schoolers are aware of their responsibilities toward their children. Their feelings are voiced by a home schooling supporter, Representative Skelly of Arizona: "Who is responsible for our children? Our youngsters weren't given to the

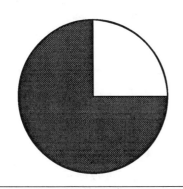

Religion was the primary reason for choosing home schooling for 75% of the families in the 1980s.

state or government. They were given by God to us as parents."

The choice of home schooling is one based on conscience. For Christians, whose belief in the Bible is unshakable, this choice means that the Bible is the foundation of all teaching. They do not want beliefs taught in school to clash with what they are teaching at home.

Every religious group has had problems in one way or another with public education. The Seventh Day Adventists are widely mentioned in connection with home schooling, but every religious denomination has supporters for home education.

For instance, many Catholics are choosing home education. A 1983 "Charter of the Rights of the Family" by the Catholic League for Religious and Civil Rights included some pro-home schooling language:

> *Parents have the right to educate their children in conformity with their moral and religious convictions. The rights of parents are violated when a compulsory system of education is imposed by the state from which all religious formation is excluded. The primary right of parents must be upheld in all forms of collaboration between parents, teachers, and school authorities.*

Other groups also have a basis for their belief in the rights of parents to home educate their children. Those groups cited in this chapter were chosen at random for specific examples, but that is not meant to imply that home schooling is exclusive to those religions.

Cathy Duffy of Garden Grove, California, summed up her her religious reasons for home schooling:

We believe that God has given parents the primary authority over their children, to raise them in a Godly and loving manner. We have the responsibility within that authority to see that our children are equipped for life with a good education. It is up to us to determine the best form that education should take for each of our children. We are free to enlist the assistance of a formal school in this task if that is the best means for us to accomplish our purpose.

The public school system very strongly reflects an attitude that discourages faith in God, love, and respect for parents and authority, and an unselfish love for mankind. These, to us, are essential aspects of our children's education. Christian schools can provide an education more in keeping with our beliefs, but they are hampered by logistics in the quality of education they can provide. (For the most part that quality far surpasses the public school system.) However, Christian schools often strive mightily to prove themselves better than their public counterparts by pushing children to achieve academic proficiency beyond their developmental capabilities. In the process children lose their love of learning, and some, unable to satisfy the system's goals, lose their self esteem.

The best learning takes place when a child is learning about something that is part of THEIR life. We can make things a part of their life by field trips, experiments, reading books, researching topics, and taking on various business ventures. Love of learning occurs when a child feels that what he is learning has value to himself and others. We try to incorporate what we learn into a cohesive whole, rather than deal with isolated subject matter.

Schools find it very difficult to implement integrated learning methods, especially as children get older. Teachers do not have the time to devote to each student to discover what will touch each of their interests. Even the best teacher cannot work as effectively as a parent with just a few children.

So, because of our religious beliefs, and also because of our desire to raise children who love to learn, we decided that the best alternative was to do it ourselves.

HOME SCHOOLS: An Alternative

RELIGIOUS BELIEFS PARENTS WANT TO PROTECT

Most people who have not studied home schooling assume that the teaching of evolution is a major concern to these parents. It is to some, but it is not the only issue cited by most religious home schoolers. It is a more widespread teaching concept that bothers them, one that covers every subject in every grade.

That teaching is the concept of *secular humanism*, or putting people in every situation before God. Parents object to this attitude in public schools. They want their children to be brought up in a God-centered life instead of a me-centered life.

I have personally found through my radio and television interviews that the general public does not understand the phrase *secular humanism*. They have heard the phrase used occasionally in the newspapers or on the television, but usually they have no idea of its real meaning. Most tell me that *humanism* must be synonymous with *humanitarian*. This leads people to mistakenly believe that *humanism* and *humanitarianism* are the same thing, so they really don't know why anyone would object to *humanism* in the schools, whether it be *secular* or not.

However, *secular humanism* refers to a philosophy of the absence of a God, according to those who have studied it. Parents objecting to humanism cite what they see as its basic tenets:

❑ Man creates God out of his own experience. (Therefore no God, only man, a form of atheism.)
❑ There are no moral absolutes.
❑ Therefore, it follows that man is his own authority and not accountable to a higher power.
❑ All forms of sexual expression are acceptable.
❑ There is no life after death.

This philosophy clashes with their basic philosophy of God as the center of their lives. They believe that humanism cultivates moral relativism, which leads to a moral vacuum, which they abhor.

HOME SCHOOLS: An Alternative

One father put it bluntly, "We parents have a right to protect our children from this godless 'religion' and the irresponsibility it promotes."

Parents citing this reason explain that religion is a way of life with them as well as a moral obligation, and that the secular humanistic philosophy is pervasive in every school subject: from early grammar to science, social science, and especially in literature courses. Since the school day takes up so many hours of every day, there is little chance for parents to counteract the teachings to which their children are exposed. A home school specialist pointed out, "Families want to be assured that the family religious dimension is not in any way shaken by a completely secular curriculum."

A newsletter from Samuel Blumenfeld, a critic of American education, was titled "The War Against Christianity in America." He believes that schools not only refrain from teaching religion, as the law is set up in this nation, but that schools actually try to eliminate Christianity in this country. He sees secular humanism as the godless religion that schools are trying to instill in our children.

Thus far, the discussion has been about implicitly anti-religious influences in the school. But parents have found even more explicit examples. One teacher overheard a counselor saying, "Christianity once served our country in a positive way, but now students today should seek other forms of religion to study and learn from." Bible stories are often placed in the same category as mythology, while students are encouraged to participate in such games as "Dungeons and Dragons." Religious home schoolers have the solution to this attack on their beliefs: Boycott the public schools.

A very serious charge against the schools was brought up during the Congressional hearing on the Hatch Amendment (discussed later). The charge was that the schools are deliberately trying to drive a wedge between parents and their children, so that the schools can replace the home-grown value system with a humanistic set of values.

Shirley Mapes of Tewksbury, Massachusetts, discovered by accident that her child was involved in a school program called Anti-Parent Pressure. The child was not supposed to take the materials home, but did so by mistake. The materials Mrs. Mapes discovered definitely shocked her.

This wedge between parent and child is allegedly done through role-playing transactional analysis, questionnaires, and surveys, where teachers delve into the private lives of their students. In other words, the teachers were playing amateur psychologists in the classroom.

Joyce Jensen, a member of the California LITE group (Let's Improve Education Today) said:

> *When these methods are used in the classroom, the student's standards, religion, family, and friends may be subject to brutal and prolonged attacks by the group. When it is all over, if one has confessed all and has had his values and ideals smashed, he may doubt if there is very much in his life worth believing or defending.*
>
> *His loyalties may have been re-aligned away from his family and church, and toward the group upon whom he has become dependent for his approval. His values of right and wrong become less important to him than his peers' approval.*

A former school teacher laid it on the line:

> *Humanism teaches that sometimes lying and stealing are acceptable. ... A value system alien from traditional values infiltrates many of the behavioral sciences textbooks. Families are the heart of America and to interfere with these values is like setting off a time bomb that will destroy America. ... Kohlberg's moral reasoning [a values clarification program] breaks down the value system (which parents spent years developing) by getting children to question their own traditional values and tell-*

> *ing them they are more mature if they develop*
> *their own value system. ... To have the values*
> *that parents spent years developing attacked*
> *and then openly stripped away is one of the*
> *greatest violations of our personal*
> *freedoms...Any teacher who participates in*
> *this program is messing with something very*
> *delicate called a child's conscience, and that*
> *is very wrong.*

The desecration of family values and outright criticism of traditional religious values prompt many families to withdraw their children from the public schools.

It's not always the curriculum that parents blame, often it's the approach to the subject. Gustavsen noted:

> *The curriculum of home schools was not*
> *significantly different than that of conven-*
> *tional schools, a fact that suggests again that*
> *it is not the courses, but the way those courses*
> *are taught, that has a negative impact on the*
> *children's moral health as perceived by the*
> *participants in this study.*

Another objection raised by religious parents is that schools institute classes designed to teach morality in a *situation ethics* approach. The teachers present cases that show a given action, and the children are to decide whether it was morally right or wrong. In several instances, children have based their judgment on their religious background, only for it to be implied that the action was considered "right in certain situations." Parents do not want schools interfering in this way, especially when the values taught in school clash with the values being taught at home.

An example of situation ethics is abortion. At school, children are often taught that abortion is moral if it involves the life of the mother or in a case of rape. When abortion issues are raised at school, parents react. They have strict beliefs on the subject, and do not want their children being taught, "This is OK if. ... " when at home they are teaching, "That is never OK."

Situation ethics are also taught through the "values clarification approach," in which students are encouraged to use role-play to make moral judgments. One widely used game is called *Life Raft*. Students are placed in groups of ten and told to pretend that they are in a life raft at sea after their ship sank. A problem exists because there is only enough room and food for nine people and one person must be thrown overboard to save the rest. The group must decide in a limited time who to throw out of the raft.

The obvious result of this "game" is that the children are taught by implication that they have the right to be the judges of the value of a human life, and to be able to value one life above another. The game is also severely damaging to the self-esteem of the person who is chosen to be thrown out of the boat. It has been reported that disabled children or minority children have been chosen based on stereotypical prejudices. Children have experienced severe trauma after playing this game. Keep in mind that role-play such as this is common in schools in every region of this nation.

Another type of values clarification approach is to ask students to rate the amount of "badness" in an act. For instance, they are asked to rate which is worse: stealing from a large store, stealing from a poor man, or parents stealing food for a starving child. The teachers are not supposed to comment on the rightness or wrongness of any answer because the idea is to get the child to think about his values, not to develop any specific ones. Therefore the child implicitly learns that whatever moral values he chooses are OK, and that there is no difference between right and wrong.

Children involved in these role-playing situations and these value clarification discussions in the classroom will eventually believe that there are *no absolutes* and that right and wrong can only be judged by what's good for themselves as individuals. The child is left in a moral vacuum.

Home schoolers object to schools teaching values contrary to their own, and even more to schools teaching a "values vacuum." Values are to be taught at home, and the only time schools should enter the picture is if they can reinforce traditional values, not destroy or confuse them. Since schools do not want to employ this position, parents feel obligated to take over the full education of their children.

The president of the Michigan Alliance of Families (a pro-family organization), Bettye Lewis, testified before the Department of Education, "If schools can't reinforce the values of the home, the schools do not have the right to deliberately destroy them."

How and where are children being involved in these values exercises? Are there courses designed just for that purpose? Yes, there have been entire courses developed just for it. The most controversial was called *MACOS: Man, A Course of Study*. After it became controversial, educators began dropping values courses from their curriculums, but began filtering values exercises into other courses of study, such as literature and social studies. Even grammar exercises show traces of values clarification influence.

Do you know what the Hatch Amendment is? In simplest terms, it's a law designed to help parents get access to the materials used in their children's curriculum in public schools.

Think about it. Why should parents need a law to look at school materials? What's so secret about them? Why can't they just walk into the school and politely ask to examine them?

It doesn't work that way any more. Life is no longer "a little town on the prairie." Schools consider their materials to be privileged information. They are also afraid that parents might find objections to them.

And rightly so! There's a whole list of objectionable materials being used. Most parents aren't aware of this because they've just never bothered.

A recent study by Dr. Paul C. Vitz of New York University entitled "Religion and Traditional Values in Public School Textbooks: An Empirical Study" found that the values most people hold dear— marriage, family, religion, heritage, and patriotism— are being excluded from textbooks. "Taken all together, these results make it clear that public school textbooks exclude the history, heritage, beliefs, and values of millions of Americans."

Parents should review their children's textbooks to see just what kind of values they are being taught. For extra help, write the Mel Gablers (address at the end of the chapter), who have a national textbook-review clearinghouse.

HOME SCHOOLS: An Alternative

I personally reviewed everything before I assigned it for my daughter. I've found it especially necessary in literature textbooks. Although some of the selections and themes studied were excellent, there were trashy parts I omitted. At the junior high and high school level, there are a lot of selections in literature books that are extremely negative in their outlook.

For instance, one story was the abridged "The Red Pony" by John Steinbeck. A boy falls in love with his pony, raises it tenderly, his parents leave it out in the rain, it dies slowly and agonizingly. That's not the worst part. In the end of the story, there's a buzzard eating the pony. The boy, in a sheer fit of violence, tears the buzzard apart with his bare hands.

This story I omitted for several reasons: for the unjustified violence, for the violence by a young person, and for the insinuation that a child can't trust his parents to do anything right. The story preceding this one I also omitted, because the theme was that a young boy ran away from home because he could not adjust to his environment.

We discuss values in our home, and we say with *certainty* what is right and wrong. So there is no reason to emphasize the negative parts of life by assigning depressing stories as a part of my daughter's curriculum.

You are what you read.
What are your children reading?

Home schoolers find other religious objections to public school curriculum. The *type* of sex education curriculum and materials is of great concern. Most parents believe that some type of biological study of reproduction is necessary, but that values concerning sex rightly should be taught at home. Birth control, abortion, premarital sex, and other moral issues are best left to the parent-child discussion.

Not only are all of these issues evaluated in schools in a situation ethics type discussion, but there are also many objectionable types of activities taking place. For instance, school children are often required to fill out questionnaires that ask how often they engage in certain types of sexual activities. There are many examples of activities that parents have told me about, but I felt that to list them here might offend the reader. The whole point, anyway, is that these activities, under the guise of "sex education," lead children to believe that "everyone is doing it" and that "it's not a matter of values, it's a matter of personal choice." These activities and discussions lead the child into an impersonal view of the sexual act and leaves him in a moral vacuum.

No wonder so many dissatisfied parents have turned to home schooling. Parents with consciences are keeping their children away from the public schools. They want their children to be fully aware of the moral implications of having sex, and not to be led into promiscuity by a curriculum that sets the wrong values, or no values at all.

Home schoolers believe in the basic philosophy of the separation of church and state, which can be accomplished only by keeping the schools from destroying the moral values taught at home. The Reagan administration was aware of the encroachment of education on the moral training of youth. On August 22, 1980, former President Ronald Reagan said:

> *As government became morally neutral, its resources have been denied to individuals professing religious beliefs and given to others who profess to operate in a value-free environment. Many of you, I'm sure, remember the controversy over the federally funded textbooks known as MACOS: Man, A Course of Study, which indirectly taught grade school children relativism, as they devised which members of their family should be left to die for the survival of the remaining ones. I don't recall the government ever granting $7 million to scholars for the writing of textbooks reflecting a religious view of man and his destiny.*

Shannon Stearns, one of the Arizona parents who testified before the U.S. Department of Education on the Hatch Amendment, said:

HOME SCHOOLS: An Alternative

This year we have taken our children out of the public schools and are home teaching them. This has proven to be a great thing for our family. We have even discovered that we can read the books and answer the questions just like teachers do. I've discovered, too, that I have much to offer them. I believe my children can withstand the temptation of drugs, alcohol, and smoking, and even bad language, but I fear that they cannot always recognize the lies that are found in the classroom at school.

Religious parents want to guide their children in the path of clear, unambiguous moral choices. It's one of the most important reasons that they are flocking to home schooling by the thousands each year.

LEGAL TEST: CONVICTION VS. PREFERENCE

Parents choosing home schooling for religious reasons have generally been protected by the courts under the First Amendment. The ruling of *Yoder vs. Wisconsin* has been widely followed. It is a case in which an Amish father was allowed to home school his children because of his religious convictions. The court applied the test of whether his convictions were sincere, or merely a preference. This test of conviction vs. preference has been used by later judges in their decisions.

Parents have had to prove their faith as being well integrated into their life practices, and not merely a subterfuge for their choice of schooling. In order to prove that their convictions were sincere, consistency in their lifestyle and actions were all examined.

The question that has been raised is whether or not non-religious home schoolers, even atheists, are also protected by the First Amendment. Home schoolers with sincere religious and moral convictions want to be protected by the Constitution, but find the religious test too limiting. People who do not adhere to any particular doctrine want the same rights as those who are following the dictates of an organized religion. Categorizing alternative beliefs has occasionally been an issue of home schooling cases as well as the test of religion.

MORAL DEVELOPMENT IN THE CHILD

Home schoolers are quite aware of the importance of moral development in their children. They know how crucial the parent-child bond is to this development.

Studies stress that a child is more likely to emulate an adult who is warm and nurturing than one who is not, and that is true in the process of moral development as well as social development. When a parent uses discipline based on love, then a child is more likely to be able to judge his own actions based on guilt or acceptance.

Knowing these principles about the development of conscience is crucial, because it leads parents to realize that physical violence does not lend itself to the proper moral development of the child, and certainly is not appropriate. This is the reason that home schoolers object to the schools' use of corporal punishment as a form of discipline. They feel that paddling is an inappropriate form of discipline, especially in the schools. Only 27 states have banned the use of corporal punishment in the schools. (See map and list next page.) The other 23 states allow physical discipline. Of these states, some have no legislation concerning the subject, which leaves the school districts to decide their own course of regulation.

Parents and child psychologists realized that the infliction of physical discipline can inhibit the development of self-esteem, can lead to physical injury, and is a short-term solution with little or no effect on behavior.

In late 1986, I stayed several weeks in the Atlanta area. During that time, there was a very sad incident in a public school. A young black youth, about 13, was paddled by the principal of his school. The next day, the young man returned to the school with his mother to discuss the paddling. Somehow, in the course of events, the child could not contain his anger, and lashed back at the principal with a sharp instrument, killing the man. This incident is just one of the many that shows that violence breeds more violence.

Barbara Fenzl, a parent of elementary school children, said, "It's a proven fact that children who are beaten are the same ones who grow up to beat their own children." EVAN-G agrees. The Committee to End Violence Against the Next

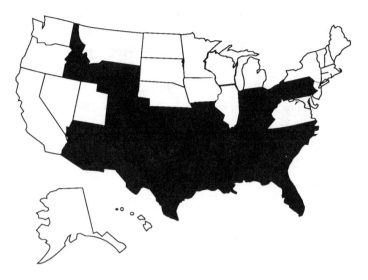

■ States allowing some form of corporal punishment in schools.
Individual districts within these states may have abolished corporate punishment.

☐ States banning corporal punishment in schools.

CORPORAL PUNISHMENT IN THE SCHOOLS

Only 27 states do not allow corporal punishment in the schools. They are:

Alaska	Massachusetts	New York	Washington
California	Michigan	North Dakota	West Virginia
Connecticut	Minnesota	Oregon	Wisconsin
Hawaii	Montana	Rhode Island	
Illinois	Nebraska	South Dakota	
Iowa	Nevada	Utah	
Maine	New Hampshire	Vermont	
Maryland	New Jersey	Virginia	

Information supplied by EVAN-G, the Committee to End Violence Against the Next Generation, Inc., 977 Keeler Avenue, Berkeley CA 94708. (510) 527-0454.

Generation is dedicated to the elimination of corporal punishment in schools. Their address is at the end of this chapter.

The most important dimensions for proper moral development are:

★Parent-child dialogue about moral issues.

★Inductive reasoning—being able to go from *if to then* in a logical fashion using examples learned from life.

★Mutual respect and cooperation between parent and child.

★Trust and affection for the role model.

These ingredients can be found only if the parents and children are able to fashion and maintain a close relationship that is unbroken by undue outside pressures.

The necessary elements to a child's moral development are found in a home school. The warmth is already there, and the consistency of the relationship adds to the child's security. Without the daily interference of school, parents can teach ethics and morals through example and dialogue. The most productive approach to helping a child discern between right and wrong is to discuss real life situations and experiences as they arise daily.

Impromptu dialogue about daily experiences is not possible in school, where everything is on a schedule. Nor is it possible for most families in this modern world, where each person goes his separate way each day, only to meet again for a few harried minutes at the end of the day before collapsing into an exhausted heap.

BUT HOME SCHOOLS CAN AND DO!

FOR MORE INFORMATION ABOUT THE SUBJECTS DISCUSSED IN THIS CHAPTER, READ THESE EXCELLENT BOOKS:

Yes, Virginia, There is Right and Wrong **by Kathleen M. Gow, PhD. Tyndale House Publishers.** This book provides an in-depth look at the moral values education in public schools.

Child Abuse in the Classroom **edited by Phyllis Schlafly. Pere Marquette Press.** This book is impossible to put down once you start reading it. It is 400 pages of excerpts from the transcript of the testimonies before the US Department of Education on the matter of the Hatch Amendment.

The testimonies are from real people, (parents and teachers), in their own words, telling about the effects of moral values education in the schools. The book will shock you, and you will never again feel the same about public education.

Classrooms in Crisis by Arnold Burron, John Eidsmoe (Attorney for Oral Roberts University and active in home schooling) and Dean Turner. Accent Books. Explains the rights of Christian parents and how they should respond to the public schools.

What Are They Teaching Our Children? by Mel & Norma Gabler. Victor Books. The Gablers lead the fight to return traditional values to textbooks. They have founded a national textbook review clearinghouse. Address below.

IMPORTANT ADDRESSES:

EVAN-G, the Committee to End Violence Against the Next Generation, Inc., 977 Keeler Ave., Berkeley CA 94708. (510) 527-0454 This group is dedicated to eliminating corporal punishment in the public schools and to ending all forms of violence against children.

The Mel Gablers, PO Box 7518, Longview TX 75607. (903) 753-5993. The Gablers, with 35 years of experience, have an extensive textbook review clearinghouse and reviews are furnished for donations. They have expanded their products to include reviews of various programs offered in schools, such as drug education (Quest and similar programs), sex education, and character education programs. In fact, the requests for information on drug education programs outweigh the requests for anything else. They have found that drug education programs are counter-productive, and more kids actually end up using drugs after the program than before. To obtain reviews, write and ask for a review of the textbook or program that you are wondering about. They also have available 30+ handbooks on various subjects of interest to home schoolers, such as one called, "Humanism and moral relativism in textbooks." A list of handbooks is available upon request. Their very informative book, *What Are They Teaching Our Children?*, is available from the Gablers. For organizations wishing case lots of this title, write the Gablers for information.

The Blumenfeld Education Letter, a newsletter by Sam Blumenfeld, a critic of American education. The April 1996 issue was titled "The California Reading Debacle: When the Incompetent Rule, the Children Suffer." Subscription price is $9 for 3 months, $18 for 6 months, and $36 per year. Available from PO Box 45161, Boise ID 83711. (208) 322-4440.

CHAPTER FIVE:
Academic Failures of Public Education

Educators claim to have fears about the academic success of home schoolers. Only 7% of the educators in my survey felt that home schooled children could receive a better education at home and 55% felt that a disadvantage of home schooling would be the lack of monitoring of a child's academic progress.

Educators seem to worry about the ability of home educated children to keep up with grade level, to have the same academic experiences, to have an equivalent curriculum, to score adequately on standardized achievement tests, to have adequate facilities, and to be taught by a qualified teacher.

The main basis for this worry, they say, is because most home schooling parents are not certified teachers. Since some of these parents were not formally educated beyond high school, educators believe they are inadequate teachers.

A Kansas educator was obviously not aware of the growing number of professional educators teaching their own children when he said:

> *It makes no more sense for a parent to attempt to educate their child, even if they have teaching credentials, than it would for them to try to diagnose and treat all forms of illness or infirmity for their child.*
>
> *Physicians refer their families to the best medical specialists; they do not attempt to treat everything themselves. Educators do the same. You won't find a professionally adequate teacher attempting to educate his or her child.*

To these complaints, John Holt replied: "When they say they're worried about home school failures, I have to be a little bit skeptical. I think they're really worried about the successes."

A North Carolina judge, in ruling against home schoolers, expressed his fear, "The state has no means by which to ensure that children at home are receiving an education."

But ensuring their child's education is exactly why many parents have withdrawn their children from public schools.

☆ In Minnesota, the Norman family withdrew their eighth grade daughter from school because she couldn't read, a fact the schools tried to ignore.

☆ A New Jersey woman brought her preschool daughter along to watch while she was a substitute teacher in a kindergarten class. Her daughter was so much further advanced in both reading and math than the class that the woman decided teaching her at home would be the only way to keep the child from being bored.

☆ A Michigan family withdrew their 9-year-old and 15-year-old sons from public schools because the older one was not challenged by the coursework, and the younger one was being pressured to learn certain facts within a time frame too rigid for him.

☆ Missouri parents are upset because "almost all the schools these days seem to set their standards according to the lowest denominator."

☆ A Colorado private school teacher worked with a home schooling family who was disenchanted with the public education system because their son's academic needs were not being met. The boy was above-average in intelligence, but was bored in school because the material was not challenging enough and the pace was too slow. The result was that his superior mind was not only going to waste, but the child was becoming emotionally disturbed. The parents explained, "A mind is a terrible thing to waste."

☆ Thousands of home schoolers are improving the education of their children by going back-to-basics or changing to a less formalized structure.

☆ Professional educators and administrators are among the ranks of people choosing home education over schools.

HOME SCHOOLS: An Alternative

Home schoolers do not all agree upon the reasons why there are so many problems in public education, any more than educators themselves can figure it out. But parents are divided into two distinct ideological groups:

1. Those who want more fundamental courses for their children, believing that only this will improve their chances at academic success: back-to-basics.

2. Those who believe that public schools are too rigid in their methods, and that less structure, such as found in a home, will lead to true learning and creative development.

A NATION AT RISK

A widely publicized 1983 report by the National Commission on Excellence in Education, *"A Nation at Risk: The Imperative for Educational Reform,"* was relentless in its list of shortcomings of American education. It cited the following among the major "indicators of the risk" to prove that American education has been slipping over the past generation:

☆ American students never scored first or second in international comparisons of student achievement.

☆ SAT scores have been in a 20-year decline. (1984 was the first year to show any increase at all in SAT scores since 1963.)

☆ One quarter of all mathematics courses taught in colleges are remedial work.

☆ The business sector, as well as the military, has to spend millions of dollars each year to educate people entering their ranks, even in the basic skills of reading, writing, and math.

The frustrating part of these statistics is that they reveal a trend toward lower academic achievement over the past generation. The report contends that: "For the first time in the history of our country, the educational skills of one generation will not surpass, will not equal, will not even approach, those of their parents." And "the average graduate of our schools and colleges today is not as well-educated as the average graduate of 25 or 35 years ago."

The answers the report supplies, unfortunately, are too simplistic and bureaucratic to be successful. The general attitude is "give students more homework, make graduation requirements tougher, pay teachers more, and the problems of public education will disappear."

These recommendations fail to see the heart of the problem, which lies in the philosophical and ideological foundations of education, and the way it has evolved as a social tool. (See Chapter 7.) The authors of the report also fail to realize that schools, as they exist, are psychologically and socially damaging to kids, and until the very basic attitudes regarding schools are changed, there will be no significant improvement.

All of the educational framework today is not going to motivate kids until educators can get inside of children's heads to see why public schools have been failing. Surface remedies treat the symptoms, not the disease.

At least this report does show concern about the present state of academic affairs in the United States. One section notes the importance of parental involvement. The section entitled "To Parents" encourages them:

> *As surely as you are your child's first and most influential teacher, your child's ideas about education and its significance begin with you. You must be a living example of what you expect your children to honor and emulate. Moreover, you bear a responsibility to participate actively in your child's education.*

EVERYONE'S CRITICIZING PUBLIC EDUCATION— IS ANYONE LISTENING?

The newspapers are never reluctant to point out the problems in education:

✪*Paducah Sun*, August 5, 1984, "It's the Public's Turn Now on Education." T. Alice McDonald, Kentucky State Superintendent of Public Instruction wrote a guest commentary in which she compares a Kentucky report in 1960 to the 1983 *A Nation at Risk* national report and finds that the disease was already evident in Kentucky in 1960.

○*Texarkana Gazette,* October 31, 1984. "New York Schools Blasted." A college president called public schools in New York a case of "shiny apples, rotten barrel" because "We have allowed a rigid, inflexible, dehumanizing educational system to develop, a system that works successfully too few times. It is the system I call the rotten barrel."

○*Daily Local News,* West Chester, Pennsylvania, September 19, 1984. "Think Tank Study Predicts a Teaching Crisis in the US." The best teachers [judged by purely academic standards, please note] are leaving the field of education for better wages and working conditions.

○*The Monitor,* McAllen, Texas, December 13, 1984. "Study: One-Fifth of Students Can't Find US on a Map." A report from the National Council for Geographical Education and the Association of American Geographers found that in 1983 tests on geography, American 12-year-olds often confused Brazil on the map for the United States. American youngsters placed fourth among an international field of eight. Their median score was 42.9 of a possible 101.

○*The Arizona Republic,* Phoenix, Arizona, March 23, 1986. "In Learning Limbo" by William Hermann, principal of St. Mary's High School in Phoenix, lashed out at our educational system: "We educate a few of our high school children for freedom and we educate a few for slavery. Most we educate for nothing at all. We learned how to educate for freedom and slavery from the ancients. Educating for nothing we seem to have invented all by ourselves."

○*News/ Sun-Sentinel,* Fort Lauderdale, Florida, January 11, 1987. "New evidence ranks the mathematical ability of American primary and high school students among the lowest of any industrialized country."

○*Fort Lauderdale News,* February 10, 1987. Headlines shout: "U.S. Schools Fail to Improve Marks." The school year 1985-1986 showed no improvement in educational achievement over the previous year. There has been little scholastic improvement since the 1983 report *A Nation at Risk.*

○*The Argus Leader,* Sioux Falls, South Dakota, April 13, 1986. "Three of four 17-year-olds are poor writers" according to a study by education writers and there is "clear cause for concern about the writing proficiency of the nation's students." The study showed that 76% of 17-year-olds could not produce an adequate piece of creative writing, 62% could not write a satisfactory piece of informative prose, and 80% of them could not write a persuasive letter.

⊙*Tempe Tribune,* Tempe, Arizona, April 2, 1989. "Arizona students lack education basics." A local publisher noted, "We graduate students from our school system who can't write, who don't read, who can't balance a checkbook, who don't know or care about history or current events, who don't know how to work hard because they're seldom asked to do so."

Since the 1983 report, a great deal of attention has been focused on improving education. Virtually every state has passed expensive educational reform legislation. Teachers' salaries have been raised substantially over the country. Yet the most recent measures of academic achievement show that there has been very little improvement since 1983. When the 1986 SAT scores were published, former Secretary of Education Terrel H. Bell said they were "the worst news we've had in a long time."

UPDATE FOR THE 1990s

In the 1990s, the problems with American public education continued to be of crisis proportions. Secretary of Education Lauro Cavazos released a national report card on education on January 10, 1990, as ordered by Congress. The results were dismal, as shown by the key findings of the document. Cavazos said, "As a nation, we should be appalled, appalled that we have placed our children in such jeopardy."

The profile of what America's high school students appear to know and are able to do is disturbing. Representative George Miller of California said bluntly, "We're launching millions of children on courses of failure."

The report gave students an "F" in reasoning skills, and most are lost when it comes to applying classroom knowledge to everyday life. The director of the report card said, "Large proportions of American students do not appear to be adequately prepared for college work, career mobility, and thoughtful citizenship."

REPORT CARD ON PUBLIC EDUCATION, 1990

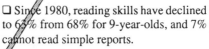

❏ Since 1980, reading skills have declined to 63% from 68% for 9-year-olds, and 7% cannot read simple reports.

❏ 42% of all 13-year-olds lack the reading skills they should have for their age level.

❏ 58% of 17-year-olds cannot read at the appropriate level. Less than 5% of 17-year-olds are reading at an advanced level, which is considered necessary for reading scientific materials, literary essays, historical documents, and other technical material.

❏ In general, children in 1988 scored as low or worse than their counterparts in 1984 in both reading and writing.

Other recent studies have continued the sad news:

✮ A study entitled "The Condition of the Professoriate: Attitudes and Trends, 1989," released November 1989 by the Carnegie Foundation for the Advancement of Teaching found that two-thirds of the faculty polled believe there has been a widespread lowering of standards of US Higher Education. And 75% of them consider their students seriously unprepared in basic skills. The survey concluded, "Public education, despite six years of reform, is still producing inadequately prepared students."

✮ The Bradley Commission, a group of distinguished historians and social studies teachers, said in a 1988 report that half of our nation's graduates never took a course in world history and 15% studied no U.S. history in high school. And recent studies show that large numbers of high school juniors enrolled in an American history course knew little of the significance of such important events as the Civil War, Reconstruction, and the Brown decision.

HOME SCHOOLS: An Alternative

✯ A 1989 report delivered to the National Governors' Association meeting in Washington D.C. showed that graduating American seniors are ignorant of the locations, cultures, and languages of other nations. Report after report has shown that American students lack basic skills in geography and history.

✯ An organization called Friends for Education released a 1989 study called "The 'Lake Wobegon Report:' How Public Educators Cheat on Achievement Tests." This report showed that there has been a great deal of cheating by teachers trying to help their students score higher on standardized tests. The teachers are desperate to raise student test scores, especially since the 1983 "Nation at Risk" report, and have been found to coach students on test questions, to give them more time than allotted, and even to alter answer sheets. This activity tends to raise student scores and averages, giving a false view of what students are actually capable of achieving. Cheating was reported in 48 states.

✯ The Carnegie Council on Adolescent Development released a 1989 report that the future of 7 million young people is in serious jeopardy because these teenagers are extremely vulnerable to school failure, substance abuse, early unprotected sexual intercourse, and other dangerous activities. The organization blames schools, saying that a "volatile mismatch exists between the organization and curriculum of middle grade schools and the intellectual and emotional needs of young adolescents."

✯ At General Motors, it was found that 20% of the workers could not read an English-language manual. At Motorola, 80% of the job applicants could not pass a fifth-grade math test. At a New York Telephone Company, 57,000 job applicants had to be tested before 2,100 were found to be qualified to be operators and repair technicians. This sad state of the low level of educational skills of American workers reflects directly on public education.

✯ An August, 1989 poll by *NBC Nightly News* found that 78% of parents say that drugs are a problem in their child's school.

HOW PUBLIC EDUCATION FAILED THEM

People are stepping forward and relating their school experiences and revealing how public education failed them. The stories are coming from superior students as well as poor ones. Both kinds of students were let down by the system.

Poor students were often kids who were turned off by the hypocrisies of public education, or who were categorized early in life as slow learners, never to escape the label.

Good students have also been disappointed by their educational life. A West Virginia woman who obtained a Ph.D. from Berkeley told about her education:

> *The problem with being a good student was that I was in it more for the grades than the learning. It didn't seem so crude or clear-cut at the time, but now it seems that my family judged me by how well I did, so grades became top priority. Even if I found the subject matter boring, useless, or offensive, I had to learn it. ...*
>
> *All I remember of history was having to memorize meaningless dates, and causes and effects of wars. I remember no women figures. The only time the past came alive was in a social studies class, where the teacher told us about the old days, how the grassy area around the school used to be fields with rabbits and other wildlife. ...*
>
> *Science didn't become real for me either. Maybe, because, again, what was taught had no connection with my limited experience.*
>
> *So I look back on decades of schooling (A.B., M.A., Ph.D.) and what do I see. A lot of it must have been irrelevant, 'cause I don't remember much. ...*
>
> *The rest of my life seems too short to re-evaluate the distortions I was taught. Now I meet a lot of intelligent, creative people who did badly in school, sometimes because of a rebellious spirit—which I admire—or learning disabilities, etc. So it seems to make more sense to burn all those old notebooks, and delve instead into the new perspectives which are becoming so much more available.*
>
> *The damage to the overachiever: I see a lot of time wasted, much distortion by male and aggressive perspectives, more passivity than I'd like to admit, lack of alternatives at the time. I PARTICULARLY REGRET THE TIME WASTED. ...*

Education in the 1990s.
Used by permission of Gary Brookins and the *Richmond Times-Dispatch*.

NEWSWEEK'S SOLUTIONS

As many "solutions" have been offered as there are problems, most of which overlook the basic premises of education in this country. *Newsweek's* cover story on September 24, 1984, was "Why Teachers Fail: How to Make Them Better." The solutions suggested were those which anyone could develop without engaging in much research or thought: tougher teacher training or easier teacher training, and more pay for educators.

Like the typical answers everyone seems to be offering today, this article concluded that the problems are either the fault of the students because of poor attitudes or the fault of careless educators. So they suggest tougher standards for both students and teachers, and believe that the problem will correct itself. At least they can be satisfied that they've tried, and ignore the problem again for a couple of years.

For some reason, no one realizes that students and teachers are mere mortals, and are reacting the way mere mortals can be expected to react under the pressures of that institutionalized myth we call American education.

I wrote to *Newsweek* criticizing the superficial answers of the attention-getting, but irrelevant article:

> *Absurd is the idea that tougher professional standards will solve the problems of public schools. The writer has taken the bureaucratic course: legislate something quick, and then we can ignore the real reasons we're having problems!*
>
> *Five years after the "problem-solving" legislation, there will be today's problems, plus a few more. Educators and legislators will put their heads together and devise an inventive solution: tougher standards for the kids. Still no improvement. Obviously, finding a solution is more of a quandary than they all suspected.*

Homeschoolers are telling me that they are pulling their children out of school because they aren't even learning the basics there. Many parents are irritated by what they call the "dumbing down" of American students.

THE ANSWERS ARE COMPLEX

The problems of public education are complex, and so are the answers to those problems. The place to start is to look at the historical foundations of education in this country (Chapter 7) and the myths that have grown up around this institution. As schools became a necessity in our minds, their function gradually changed, and then our relationship to them changed also. Schools have become the workplace of our youth, as intimidating and unwelcoming as any sweatbox factory. In changing so much, they have become bad places for kids socially and psychologically.

Critics of public education have been pointing out these fundamental truths for years, but a solution involves the intangibles, such as a change in attitudes, and a change in the way we view kids and learning and the purpose of schools. That's difficult for most administrators to grasp. They have trouble understanding the things they can't put on paper. It's easier for them to try to solve problems with new rules and regulations that can be written and shown to everyone. Then they can say, "See! We've done everything we can to work on the problems. Regulations numbers 255 through 379 will clear up everything."

In spite of the complexity of the problems and the enormous changes that would be needed, vast improvements could be made by:

▼**More parental involvement.** As a society, we have turned our backs on our children and on what's happening to them in schools. Kids come home each day with a handful of papers. We say, "That's nice," and go back to what we were doing. Most parents are unaware of exactly what is happening each day and how their child is progressing, or even *if* he is progressing. Americans have babies, nurture them as long as it's convenient, and then automatically turn them over to preschool and school.

Gary Bauer, of the US Department of Education, appeared on a *MacNeil/Lehrer News Hour* on November 13, 1985, to discuss the possibility of a voucher system for American schoolchildren. One of the reasons he supported the proposed system is "because it would put parents back in the driver's seat for their children's education." He stated,

> Parental involvement is the number one factor in determining the success of a child's education.

Orientals in this country are academically successful. This success has been credited to the great amount of parental involvement in their children's education.

Now attention is turning to the Japanese system of education, known for producing more engineers than American schools. Japanese high schools also graduate 90% of their students, compared to 70% in the U.S. A high school education in Japan is equivalent to half of a college education here.

A 1987 report by the U.S. Department of Education called, "Japanese Education Today" explains why there is a much higher achievement by Japanese students: "The Japanese child's first teachers and most important supporters are the parents, primarily the mother. ... The educational role of home and family is as fundamental a determinant of Japanese success in education as any factor could be."

▼**Less red tape for teachers.** Professional educators should not be bogged down with mountains of paperwork. It's not their function. It's the reason that little time can be spent with students. Teachers have to show results on paper for their superiors, and this, in turn, causes pressure on students to perform like trained rats.

Less attention, not more, should be given to academic results that can be measured. Studies have shown that certain intangibles, like creativity, and true learning (explained later), are difficult to measure. A better question is, why try to measure these things?

Fewer records to keep would mean less classification of students, which in turn could help prevent turning out clones. If teachers didn't record such idiocies as "dyslexic," "perceptually handicapped," "unmotivated," "slow learner," then these children would never have to be put into an inescapable category.

▼**Hiring teachers on the basis of their ability to elicit positive responses from students rather than on the basis of their academic background.** Just as creativity cannot be measured, neither can good teaching. A Ph.D. is more likely a symbol of someone who can be a good student than an indicator of a good teacher.

Methodology coursework cannot make good teachers. The main purpose of these courses is to show how to draw rigid lesson plans, how to run audio-visual equipment, and how to keep beautiful attendance records. There is no evidence that certified teachers produce better results than uncertified teachers. So why the fuss?

▼**More emphasis on true learning , rather than rote memorization.** Explanation follows.

TRUE LEARNING

So what is true learning? Schools see learning as a measurable trait: the number of facts a student can memorize; a test score; class rank. Of course that leads right back to the problems of schools, so obviously that's not a reliable definition of true learning.

True learning is a paradox; more complicated, yet simpler than numerical measures. It's more complicated because it's an abstraction, but it's simpler because even babies can do it. Learning is making a complex world more understandable.

Child development professionals have observed how babies approach their world. Curiosity is a natural trait and it doesn't need to be learned. Curiosity leads babies to observe, manipulate, and explore their environment. They are avid experimenters. In the first year alone, a baby learns how to sit, crawl, walk, say a few words, and communicate nonverbally. And no one puts him on a schedule!

Learning is as natural to children as growing.They learn because they want to, not because they are forced. This true learning style would continue throughout life, except that we force kids to go to school. Schools put them on an inflexible "learning" schedule. Suddenly, teachers feel they need to "motivate" kids to learn, whereas before you couldn't stop them from learning if you wanted to.

Asking questions is essential to learning. Every parent knows that one of his 3-year-old's favorite words is "Why?" Good parenting involves answering these questions now, not tomorrow, and in a way that is easy for the child to understand. The child is learning, the parent is teaching. But had the parent forced the child to sit and listen to that same information without the child first asking, then it's a good bet the time would have been wasted. People can learn when they're ready, and readiness can be expressed by questions.

"Reading Readiness" is a favorite buzz-phrase for professional educators. It means that the child has distinguished between certain shapes, and can tell the order or arrangement of objects. This is supposedly a good indication of whether a child is able to distinguish one letter of the alphabet from another, and whether the difference between "s-a" and "a-s" means anything to him yet. Children are customarily tested for reading readiness in preschool or kindergarten. Then educators "know" whether or not that child is ready to read.

Home schoolers have found all of that nonsense unnecessary. Most of them have found that their youngsters are ready to learn to read when they start asking questions like, "What does that spell?" or "What does that mean, Mommy?" Children's natural style of learning will lead them to ask questions about signs, newspapers, cereal boxes—*when they're ready*.

Most educators don't like to answer questions; it messes up their schedules.

Teacher at a museum: Don't start asking questions, or we'll never get through.

HOME SCHOOLS: An Alternative

Parents in a home schooling situation are available and eager to answer questions. A South Dakota minister saw the following:

> One Sunday I was entertained in a farm home of a member of our rural church. I was impressed by the intelligence and good behavior of the only child in the home, a 4-year-old boy.
>
> Then I discovered one reason for the child's charm. His mother was at the kitchen sink, washing the intricate parts of the cream separator when he came to her with a magazine. "Mother," he asked, "what is this man in the picture doing?"
>
> To my surprise, she dried her hands, sat down on a chair and taking the boy in her lap, she spent the next ten minutes answering his questions. After the boy left, I commented on her having interrupted her chores to answer the boy's questions, saying, "Most mothers wouldn't have bothered."
>
> She told me, "I expect to be washing cream separators for the rest of my life, but never again will my son ask me that question."
>
> Thank God for mothers and fathers who care and take the time.

Another aspect of learning is thinking. Seems ambiguous, but it's not. We have to learn analytical thinking, and that should be a major goal for teachers.

> The aim of education should be to teach us rather how to think, than what to think—rather to improve our minds, so as to enable us to think for ourselves than to load the memory with the thoughts of other men.
>
> **James Beattie, 1735-1803**
> **Scottish poet**

The ability to reason, to organize, and to figure out the intentions behind men's words, all need to be learned. A major purpose of learning should be to help the student learn to function in the world. Curiosity leads to questions, which leads to answers, which eventually leads to more questions, and then all of this information needs to be put into a logical order in the mind, so that it makes sense and will be useful to the learner. Analytical thinking follows when the student has assimilated enough information to be critical or skeptical about the information that he has received. Exploration beyond that point is reasoning. Major breakthroughs in science and technology come from this exploration: minds that see beyond "impossible" to "possible" because they have learned to reason, organize, and analyze.

> *The object of teaching a child is to enable him*
> *to get along without his teacher.*
> **Elbert Hubbard, 1856-1915**
> **American writer, editor**

Unfortunately, educators today are making students more dependent, not less. John M. Mason, an American theologian in the late 18th century, warned educators:

> *Don't fall into the vulgar idea that the mind is a*
> *warehouse, and education but a process of stuffing it*
> *full of goods.*
> *The aim of education should be to convert the mind*
> *into a living fountain, and not a reservoir. That which*
> *is filled by merely pumping in, will be emptied by*
> *pumping out.*

So eloquently stated. Every student knows how to cram for an exam. Two days later, he may have his "A" but little true knowledge. Educators force students to behave this way because the system forces them to measure and rate, but it falls short of real teaching.

Haven't you heard the expression, "When you haven't got an education, you just have to use your brains!" That paradox is only true because of the way schools are set up to detour around thinking instead of meeting the challenge squarely.

The exchange and development of ideas is another part of true learning. Society is a multi-faceted organism, and so are the elements of personality. Exploring the differences can be exciting!

HOME SCHOOLS: An Alternative

Let our teaching be full of ideas. Hitherto it has been stuffed full of facts.

Anatole France, 1844-1924
French novelist

The majority of educators in my survey, 78% (Chapter 11) felt that home schools could not provide the stimulation of ideas available in the classroom. It's ironic that schools have this potential, yet rarely take advantage of it.

Real teaching swims parallel to real learning, helping only to coach, direct, and praise, but it cannot overpower learning. If it does, two swimmers drown.

Somewhere in time, educators began to believe that they have a monopoly on teaching and learning. They made parents feel that only certified teachers are smart enough to impart knowledge.

Well, take heart, home schoolers. That's just not true. Actually there is no evidence whatsoever that certified teachers are better than uncertified ones. And some of the best teachers of children are other children. They don't have to worry about the myths that say that they can't teach each other.

An interesting idea is testing teachers. In March 1983, 3,200 Houston teachers took the Pre-Professional Skills Test—the one students have to take if they want to become teachers. The results: 44% of the teachers failed reading, 46% failed math, and 26% failed the writing portion of the exam. The conclusions that some people reached was that those teachers were incompetent, but a better conclusion is that tests are irrelevant. So why should students constantly be subjected to testing, then categorized accordingly?

Questions, Thinking, Ideas.

All of these elements are part of the structure of learning. Together they nail it solid. Without them, the structure falls apart. Public schools are failing to provide these essential elements.

HOME SCHOOLS: An Alternative

It is, in fact, nothing short of a miracle that modern methods of instruction have not entirely strangled the holy curiosity of inquiry; for this delicate little plant, aside from stimulation, stands mainly in need of freedom; without this it goes to wrack and ruin without fail. It is a very grave mistake to think that the enjoyment of seeing and searching can be promoted by means of coercion and a sense of duty. To the contrary, I believe that it would be possible to rob even a healthy beast of prey of its voraciousness, if it were possible with the aid of a whip, to force the beast to devour continuously even when not hungry, especially if the food, handed out under such coercion, were to be selected accordingly.

Einstein

Home schools are doing better, as I show in the next chapter.

FOR MORE READING IN THE TOPICS IN THIS CHAPTER, CHECK THE FOLLOWING:

A Nation at Risk: The Imperative for Educational Reform, the report by the National Commission on Excellence in Education. US Department of Education, 1983. Available for $4.50 from the **Superintendent of Documents, US Government Printing Office, Washington DC 20402.**

NEA: Trojan Horse in American Education by Samuel Blumenfeld, Para-digm Company, 1984.

All of John Holt's books, listed in the Bibliography.

CHAPTER SIX:
Academic Advantages of Home Schools

Exploring the problems of public education and then searching for solutions would take volumes. Critics have been working over the subject for years, with no definitive answers. But the fact remains that until improvements are made, parents do have a choice. Home schools have many obvious academic advantages:

1. **Parents have 100% involvement with their children,** and are not side-tracked by the red tape binding educators (except for the paperwork required by local officials). They can devote their attention to their own child's education. They can daily monitor the progress of the children. Parents like their children as people, so the teacher-pupil relationship is solid, secure, and warm. This emotional bond is an important part of the requirements for learning.

Forty-one percent of the educators in my survey realized that parents in a home school can monitor academic progress better than a teacher because parents have more time for individual attention.

2. **Parents can choose the amount of structure that is best suited for them and their children.** Each program can be individualized to suit the needs and interests of each child. Each child can progress at his own rate, instead of the rate of the group. Learning by experience can easily be provided. There is no need to push any child into material that he is not ready for.

3. **Parents won't categorize their kids,** classifying them as "slow learners" or other

handicapping labels. Each child will be treated as an individual, not as a set of records. Grades will be less important than true learning.

4. Learning is a year-round experience, and the home school provides this. The atmosphere in the home will be one where learning is exciting, not painful. The continuum of experience is an important factor in learning and need not be interrupted by the calendar.

5. Learning can be a "hands-on" experience. In the home, active physical involvement with learning creates a bond between the child and the subject. This type of involvement occurs occasionally in schools, but not often enough. Manipulation of materials has always been acknowledged as a key factor in successful learning. Maria Montessori, who developed the Montessori method, said:

> *We discovered that education is not something which the teacher does, but that is a mutual process which develops spontaneously in the human being. It is not acquired by listening to words, but in virtue of experience in which the child acts in his own environment.*

HOME SCHOOL SUCCESSES

✍Home schooled students have been accepted at Harvard, Yale, Antioch, Texas A & M, William & Mary, Brigham Young University, California State Universities, and many other prestigious institutions of higher learning.

✍Eighteen-year-old Grant Colfax of Booneville, California (a rural area) was taught at home for 11 years. He was accepted for college entrance at Harvard and Yale. He caught the attention of the media, and was featured on *NBC Evening News*. He chose to go to Harvard. The admissions officer, Robert Cashion, said to the press after interviewing Grant: "The young man struck me as someone who really enjoyed the learning process. It was refreshing to see." Grant excelled in Harvard, and then was followed there by younger brothers, also home schooled. Now the Colfax family is known nationwide, and has a book called *Homeschooling for Excellence*.

HOME SCHOOLS: An Alternative

✍️Amy Hovenden, 14, started studies at Brigham Young University, the youngest freshman to ever be accepted by the university. She is the oldest of 9 children who were educated by their parents in Utah-based "Sterling Academy," a home school.

✍️In 1976, Mark Edwards enthusiastically began college at California State University at Hayward. He was only 16-years-old and had passed the state GED exam (high school equivalency.) Two years later, at 18, he was a junior at the University of California at Berkeley; his younger brother, Matthew, 14, was a freshman at Holy Name College in Oakland. They had been home schooled.

✍️Charles Baker, educated at home from grades 6 through 12, graduated from Texas A & M with a degree in biomedical science and planned to go on to either veterinary or medical school.

✍️Thom Peterson of Chanhassen, Minnesota, was educated at home for 7 years. He was not only ready to go to college at age 17, but he had also participated in the campaign of a Senate candidate.

✍️In Virginia, home schooled Darrin Geisy was accepted at the college of his choice. He also appeared in the TV miniseries *George Washington* as George's brother, Charles.

✍️In Deerfield, Massachusetts, Joan Beasley removed her sixth grade son from public school for one year. When he returned to public school, he joined a junior high honors program, his reading level had reached 12th grade,his math level had reached 9th grade.

✍️Tom Ingersoll of Sheffield, Massachusetts, was home educated until he was sixteen, when he decided that he wanted to go to high school. He immediately became one of the school's best students and made the honor roll.

✍️The Ruzicka children of Arizona have been home schooled for 3 years. Each year they have been tested with the same test administered to public and private school children. The Ruzicka children have tested out well above their age and grade levels.

✍️A Vermont boy, home schooled for several years, was accepted by Bard College. He was given a full scholarship.

✍️The University of Texas at San Antonio accepted a 16-year-old girl who had been home schooled.

HOME SCHOOLS: An Alternative

✍Home schooling has helped students attain grade level by instilling in them confidence. One young man, in a LD (learning disabilities) class was taken home for six months. When he returned to school, he jumped two grades.

✍Home schoolers generally score at least two grade levels above their peers on standardized tests. Quite often they score three and four grade levels higher. Students who return to public education after a few years of home instruction are often put in "rapid achievement" classes—the classrooms for gifted students. One home schooling proponent believes that 99% of the families teaching their own kids are doing so much better than the average school system. That's an impressive record.

HOME SCHOOL STUDIES

Homeschooling is becoming so widespread in the United States that there have been numerous studies on their outcomes.

✍One study reported in the *Phi Delta Kappan* showed that homeschooled children score higher on standardized tests than did their peers in the Los Angeles Public Schools.

✍The South Dakota Department of Education, 1992, found that homeschooled fourth grade children scored at the 81st percentile in the composite scores on the Stanford Achievement Test.

✍Tennesse Department of Education, 1986, reported that homeschooled students outscored public school students consistently. The homeschooled children rated in the top 3% in math, top 4% in spelling, top 1% in listening skills, and top 6% in environmental knowledge.

✍Another study by *Phi Delta Kappan* reported that a majority of two thousand homeschooled students achieved notable progress in academic, attitudinal, and motivational progress.

✍National Home Education Resource Institute, 1990, surveyed over 1400 families, and found that homeschooled students scored at least 30 points higher than national averages on standardized achievement tests *in every subject tested.*

EXPERTS ON LEARNING

Some people are not easily convinced about the academic success of home schools. For them, I have included this section about theories on cognitive development, as proof of the advantages of home schools.

Two schools of thought exist on cognitive development. The behaviorists stress the effects that exterior forces, such as stimulus and response, have on learning. The psychoanalytics believe that the internal forces, such as hidden impulses, are more important to learning.

One behaviorist studied reinforcers that promote learning. B.F. Skinner considered operant conditioning to be very important in the complex learning process. This conditioning is created through positive and negative reinforcements: rewards and punishments.

Three types of reinforcements play a role in learning: basic reinforcements (food, physical comfort) are more effective in young children, complex or symbolic reinforcements (college diploma) are effective for adults, and social reinforcements (praise, time spent with loved one) are powerful at any age.

Timing is crucial when reinforcers are used to promote learning. Rewards must be immediate when used for young children. Later, rewards can be used less often and for larger accomplishments. For example, a 6-year-old learning to read might be given a piece of fruit after sounding out each word, but after he learns how to read, a reward after each book is sufficient. Eventually, praise will be enough.

Developmental experts who subscribe to Skinner's theories on learning can see advantages to home schooling. There is immediate reward for achievement. Parents can see accomplishments as they happen, so there is an immediacy of feedback. The responses take place within minutes, instead of days as in the typical classroom. Teachers have so many students and so much paperwork that they can rarely take the time to give individual praise. Children desperately need that praise to build their self-esteem. In school, usually only the best students receive praise, the rest are ignored and begin to feel cheated or stupid. Most simply give up.

Psychoanalytic experts also have their theories on cognitive development. Jean Piaget, the Swiss psychologist, is the most widely quoted of these. His ideas encompass the following:

✔The rate of cognitive development is different for each child. Each stage of development evolves gradually and depends on the child's individual experiences. A child should not be pushed through the process.

✔The classroom should be a place where children can experiment and explore. They should not be forced to learn lists of facts in rigid time frames.

✔A system that compares one child's scores against another's is damaging to the child's learning process.

✔Ideas, not facts, are important to learn, especially from the ages of 6-11. Materials should be available in the classroom for the development of ideas.

Other developmental experts have further explained Piaget's ideas. David Elkind wrote that "from the Piagetian perspective, there are optimal periods for growth of particular mental structures that cannot be rushed."

Eleanor Duckworth, another expert in this field, stated:

> *It is almost impossible for an adult to know exactly the right time for a given question for a given child—especially for a teacher who is concerned with 30 or more children. The children can raise the right question for themselves when the setting is right.*

These psychoanalytical theories on learning show more obvious advantages of home schooling:

✎Parents don't need to force learning on a preconceived schedule. They have the flexibility to help the child explore ideas when he is ready.

✎Parents can provide as much or as little structure as the child needs. The most important thing for parents to provide is an environment conducive to learning and materials to pique the child's curiosity.

✎The child will not daily be compared to his peers. His learning process will be uniquely his own.

✎Ideas can be developed through parent-child interaction instead of just rote memorization. For instance, looking at history as something that happened to real people, instead of just learning dates and names of documents.

Dr. Raymond Moore, a child psychologist and a home school proponent, and his wife Dorothy, a reading specialist, have studied the impact of early childhood education. From their studies they have developed ideas on the ideal learning environment. They have found that early learning heavily depends on a self-esteem gained through approval by parents, on exploration through curiosity, and on manipulation of materials. This learning will be inhibited if the child feels fear, disapproval, uncertainty, passivity through too much TV viewing, or is put too early into an environment of structured learning, such as preschool. A structured approach can lead to boredom for young children.

Dr. Moore stresses that the most important factor in cognitive development is the quality of home and family. This is always number one! He agrees with Piaget that rates vary for children's intellectual growth.

Early school entrance, between the ages of 3 and 8, can damage the learning process for children. Before they can really learn, they must have a positive sense of self-worth, developed through a close parental relationship.

The Moores are so concerned about people pushing their children into school too early that they have tried to persuade parents to teach their children at home, at least in the early years. Parents can contribute to their children's future intellectual growth by keeping them at home until at least ten.

A school psychologist in Pennsylvania, Joel Eron, studied the effects of early school entrance. He found that a preponderance of the children who are classified by schools as learning disabled were at the young end of the spectrum when they started first grade. In other words, children who are even a few months less mature when they enter first grade are more likely to develop reading difficulties. Schools don't often wait for children to be "ready" (in spite of their techniques of trying to prove "Reading Readiness") before they start to teach reading. As a result, they create failures of students who could succeed if only schools were more patient.

HOME SCHOOLS: An Alternative

The shocking conclusion is one that home schoolers have already discovered—children can not only be intellectually stifled in schools, but they can actually be shut out of the learning process forever simply by school's pushiness.

The academic advantages of home education are obvious. The successes of home schoolers are obvious. The choice for a parent who really cares about his child's education is obvious!

FOR MORE READING ON THE TOPICS DISCUSSED IN THIS CHAPTER, CHECK THE FOLLOWING:

"The Having of Wonderful Ideas," an article by Eleanor Duckworth in the *Harvard Educational Review,* 1972, Volume 42, pages 217-231.

Children and Adolescents: Interpretive Essays on Jean Piaget by David Elkind. NY: Oxford University Press, 1974.

How Children Learn by John Holt. NY: Dell, 1967.

The Underachieving School by John Holt. NY: Pitman Publishing Company, 1969.

Better Late Than Early by Raymond and Dorothy Moore. NY: Reader's Digest Press, 1975.

School Can Wait by Raymond and Dorothy Moore. Provo UT: Brigham Young University Press, 1979.

All of Piaget's and Skinner's books listed in the Bibliography.

All of Skinner's books listed in the Bibliography.

CHAPTER SEVEN
The Historical, Political, & Ideological Issues

A glimpse at the historical foundations and premises of public education in the United States shows the rationale behind the growing number of alternative schools, including home schools. Historical perspectives can give an idea of where education is, and why. To see where we are now, and where we're going, a good idea is to see where we've been and how we managed to get here.

Why do we have public education in the United States? What philosophy propelled compulsory attendance laws? These issues affect home schools and the people who run them. A quick study of the history of American public education answers these questions.

COLONIAL TO REVOLUTIONARY WAR PERIOD

The idea of popular education, or education for the masses, had its roots in the Reformation in Europe. For a Bible authority to maintain its influence, the people had to have Bible literacy. They had to be taught to read the Bible in order for the Reformation to continue. It was not genuinely an effort for mass elevation, but an effort to change the type of control used on people. The new authority was to be a "rational" one, to replace one of superstition.

The same need for Bible literacy motivated the Puritans in Massachusetts Bay Colony when they instituted their public education system. In 1789, Massachusetts entered the Union and enacted the first comprehensive state school laws in this budding nation. At the time, compulsory education was as much a means of religious discipline as it was a means of ensuring literacy. The two ideas were inseparable.

The designers of the Constitution and early American statesmen were also advocates of education for the masses. Such figures as John Adams and Thomas Jefferson were convinced that citizens of the newly-formed country needed education to help the transformation from colonies to states take place. Free men needed knowledge to make decisions concerning their government.

Jefferson believed that education was important not only for decision-making, but also for the education of moral elevation. Thus the philosophy behind the genesis of public education in America was not only religious, but political as well.

THE 1800s SECULAR TRANSFORMATION

The 19th century saw a great change in the philosophy behind public education. Instituted in Massachusetts for Bible literacy, the idea of education for everyone spread among the states, but for different reasons. As the common school system was established, a tax structure was created to support the institution. Justification of the tax burden was necessary, so proponents argued that government schools were necessary to teach the young to respect America's political, moral, and religious institutions.

The public education movement gained impetus from supporters such as Robert Dale Owens and Horace Mann, who gave the movement its thrust toward a secular notion of progress. Thus, public education, first a disciplinary tool for religion, became a disciplinary tool for social change and democracy.

Mann was convinced that there was a close relationship between education and national progress. He called universal education the "great equalizer of men" and the "balance wheel of social machinery."

Education, according to Mann, was the tool with which democracy was achieved. Shaping individual men would shape a nation. Through public education, poverty would disappear, class lines would become extinct, and all evils common to man would cease to exist. The new democracy would become a type of social utopia heretofore only dreamed about.

HOME SCHOOLS: An Alternative

Schoolhouses are the republican line of fortification.

Horace Mann

The 1800s saw the secularization of American education. As William Torrey Harris said in 1867, "The spirit of American institutions is to be looked for in the public schools to a greater degree than anywhere else."

Education is the only political safety.

Horace Mann

INDUSTRIAL REVOLUTION'S EFFECT ON EDUCATION

The growth of factories and the number of people working in them were compelling forces in the institution of compulsory attendance laws in many states. The idea was to protect the young from forced labor. Child labor laws were also enacted at this time.

Since the basic idea for these compulsory attendance laws was protection, few people questioned their legitimacy. Not many people looked upon it as a loss of educational freedom, which indeed it was.

No longer were people allowed the freedom to choose the type of education they wanted for their children. They were told by law that there was a *correct* way to educate their children. If they did not like their local public schools, and they could not afford a private school, they were stuck. Laws prohibited them from teaching their children at home, to "protect" the kids.

The secularization of public schools continued throughout the industrial transformation. Schools were propelled not only by a need to teach children academically, but also to mold their political, moral, and social characters. The building of children's characters was deemed the school's duty.

John Dewey continued the philosophy of Horace Mann, that schools were a necessary tool for democracy. Individuals needed to be shaped in such a way that they would accept and fit into the institutions. Ignored was the simple idea that freedom was lost when public education became an institution by law. Forgotten was the importance of the family in the development of an individual's personality and values.

> *The teacher is engaged, not simply in the training of individuals, but in the formation of the proper social life.*
>
> **John Dewey**

Another educator, Dr. Frank Cody, expressed the popular opinion about school's importance as an institution:

> *The development of desirable traits and characteristics—that intangible something we style personality—is the chief work of the school.*

Thus 1800s educators expanded the importance of the school, from academics to social, and even into the area best regarded as belonging to the family: the role of shaping the individual.

20th CENTURY EDUCATION

By the 20th century, public education had already become an institution. One by one, the states enacted compulsory attendance laws. Freedom of choice was limited to private or public schools, or in rare instances, privately hired tutors. The trend of schools was still to teach the young to fit into the American way of life.

Several events in this century strengthened public education's hold on American's young. World Wars I and II frightened defense-minded citizens, who, bound together by fear, believed that public schools would keep a foothold on democracy.

The Depression was also a fearful time for most Americans. The anxieties of those lean years led people to believe that education by established institutions would help their children find high-paying jobs so that they would never again have to agonize over poverty.

HOME SCHOOLS: An Alternative

McCarthyism also played on people's fears. Individuals who didn't fit properly into the American mold were automatically branded "Communist" by their neighbors. This scare was a great plus to schools, giving them the chance to show how well they "Americanized" children.

By the middle of the 20th century, schools were deeply entrenched in the minds of Americans as an absolutely necessary institution, and people were convinced that they could not survive without public education.

Schools became big political machines, whether or not most parents realized it. A 1960 report by the Kentucky House of Representative's Special Committee to Investigate Education said, "A powerfully entrenched political machine can grow within a framework of the local school system, and we believe that this had, in fact, occurred in the greater number of Kentucky counties."

Some of the teachers in my survey (Chapter 11) are among those who wish schools to continue to be a social tool. Eloise Owens of Pennsylvania said, "I believe in most situations, the disadvantages to home instruction far outweigh the advantages. In a democratic society, we need an enlightened citizenry who will be able to interact intelligently in society for their own development as well as for the welfare of all."

Sounds more like socialistic sentiments to me, when people say that individuals exist for the welfare of the society. The term *democracy* was meant by our founding fathers to be the type of atmosphere where the individual could survive *as an individual,* without having to conform to the expectations of the group. Individuals must not infringe on the rights of others, but they also should be allowed to decide whether or not to join the institutions.

Public schools breed and encourage the values of the people who control them. If the people in charge want to promote materialism, then materialism is taught implicitly.

The social movements of the 1960s awakened America's slumbering awareness of the growing problems in public education. Critics have written numerous books on the basic faults of the system. In any public or university library, there is a large section on criticism of public education that has been written within the last 25 years. In fact, every week this publisher receives manuscripts about the

HOME SCHOOLS: An Alternative

> **Every week we hear from professional educators that they are "fed up with the system."**

problems of American education from educators and PhDs who are "fed up with the system"—their own words.

Has anyone been listening to these critics? Apparently not, because the system continues to compound the problems.

Schools are in a state of future shock, and are creating individuals who go passively through their halls and then smack into the world to catch their very own case of future shock.

Future shock exists in schools because they have frozen into rigidity instead of responding to the changing society. Confronted with all of the choices of how they could improve, schools have done nothing. Basically, public education is the same as it was 50, even 100 years ago.

The frozen institution molds people who are far from ready for the world that awaits them. They go into their own case of future shock because they are unable to adjust to a world that is radically different from the world that schools taught them to believe in. Some of these graduates withdraw from the world, and others respond by continuing to act as though the beliefs they had been taught really did exist, leaving them at the mercy of reality.

Another factor of public education today is the strength of its union, the National Education Association (NEA). Even the Department of Education finds the NEA a formidable foe. The NEA has opposed a suggested voucher system, which would allow parents the freedom to use their tax dollars for whatever type of education they would choose for their children, whether it be public, private, or home schools. The NEA fears that a multitude of parents would leave public education if allowed the choice openly and encouraged to look at the options. Therefore, they argue that the tax dollars (all $120 billion of them a year) belong only to public schools.

In spite of the attitudes that filter down from the top, some educators realize that options are an inevitable part of the future of American education. Donna Soldano of California said:

HOME SCHOOLS: An Alternative

Home schooling, in fact, all alternative school-
ing, must be an integral part of our future. The
educational institution will need to be flexible
to meet multi-dimensional objectives.

OBJECTIONS OF HOME SCHOOLERS

Home schoolers object to schools institutionalizing and promoting values. These parents want to be the most influential people in their children's lives. A
Missouri parent said, "We're being suffocated with unwanted help from government
experts who pretend to know more than parents do about raising their own children."

Parents don't want their kids to become robots of the state. They want to
teach their children their own ideals, not necessarily what the government wants to
promote. These parents are not anarchists, but rather realists who see certain values,
like consumerism, being pushed in schools because of government influence. They
believe in patriotism and loyalty, but not in state-regulated value systems. An attorney
for home schoolers said, "We're getting more and more oriented to the state and less
toward the family."

An overwhelming majority of home schoolers, 82%, believe that there is
too much government interference in public education, in spite of a supposed laissez-
faire policy of politics on schools. Instead, the influence of the present administration
(whatever that may be) is heavily felt by the values propagated in the classroom.

**What are the types of ideologies learned in the classroom to which
parents object?**

1. **Consumerism**—the schools creating consumers, to buy the products of companies
   owned by "big money." Teaching kids that everything is disposable, that it can
   be replaced by buying another. The "keep up with the Joneses" attitude is heavily
   felt by children in school.

2. **Conformity to the marketplace**—designing workers for the labor force instead
   of teaching students to think independently and creatively. Everything is de-

signed to lead students to a particular niche in society, at an age where he may not yet know what he wants to do.

3. **Job orientation**—leading young people to believe that their entire role in life is *to hold a job.* Rarely are students encouraged to be entrepreneurs, artisans, or anything that doesn't fit into a neat little job package.

4. **Loss of independence**—creating dependence on other people and institutions. The educational institution has led the rumor that only certified teachers are able to teach children, that only specialists in each profession are allowed any knowledge about the field. That attitude puts tunnel vision on the child's perspective about learning.

5. **Emphasis on numerical measures**—leads to lack of concern for personal growth. Also encourages kids to think that something is good only if it can be measured with a number, such as thinking that the amount of money a person earns is more important than the person himself. This attitude is very dehumanizing. The person begins to emphasize dollars, credit card numbers, and rank. He feels valuable only if he is number 1, has a $200,000 home, a $20,000 car, 15 credit cards, $12,000 credit line, and is ranked at least number 17 in his company chain of command. More seriously, he starts thinking about his family as numbers: wife number 2, child number 3, and alimony payment number 22.

6. **Uniformity**—all students must fit into the same mold. All graduates must have the same design.

7. **Information vulnerability**—inability to think analytically, but capable of spouting statistics or quotes as critical proof. Many people cannot think for themselves or form their own opinions, depending instead upon what is deemed by society to be correct or government's statistics. Unless something has been stated in school as "fact," many people will not even consider the alternative. They become narrow-minded and opinionated because they have not learned how to analyze

information. Processing new data is too difficult because they never learned how to do it. Instead, they will believe anything printed in the newspapers and anything on newscasts.

8. **Hypocrisy**—teaching about democracy while taking away the student's freedom of choice. Certain practices of schools are also hypocritical, such as not allowing parents and children to view school records, but giving easy access of these records to the police, the military, the government, and employers. Other objectionable practices are compulsory psychological testing, and filling records with labels, such as "slow learner" or "uncooperative."

9. **Class distinctions**—schools promote rather than erase these categories. Kids are taught to respect certain professions and to try to attain that status. If a certain type of work is not considered respectable by the schools, especially if it does not require many years of higher education and the passing of rigid requirements, then kids are taught that it is unworthy. Money is respected, regardless of its implications. A Colorado parent said that public education is "a class institution [designed] to impart class values on working people so they will think the way they should to fit into a working-class world."

Schools have evolved from the colonial religiously oriented education to the modern institution surrounded by myth and protected by government. Confronted by these giant vessels of paradoxes, many parents have chosen to educate their children at home. Home schools give parents the chance to teach their children the values they wish them to internalize.

FOR MORE STUDY ON THE HISTORY AND IDEOLOGY OF
AMERICAN EDUCATION, READ THE FOLLOWING:

Is Public Education Necessary? Samuel Blumenfeld. Paradigm Press, PO Box 45161, Boise ID 83711.

NEA: Trojan Horse in American Education. Samuel Blumenfeld. Paradigm Press, PO Box 45161, Boise ID 83711.

American Writers on Education Before 1865. Abraham Blinderman. Boston: Wayne Pub., 1975.

The Transformation of the School. Lawrence A. Cremin. NY: Alfred A. Knopf, 1961.

Teaching as a Subversive Activity. Neil Postman & Charles Weingartner. NY: Dell, 1969.

CHAPTER EIGHT
Legal Aspects

The laws concerning home schooling have been generally confusing, ambiguous, and unsatisfactory. State governments have the authority to legislate over education in general, so there is a great deal of variance across the nation. Some state laws rigidly control home schools; others are more permissive.

The range is so great that even rigid states can seem permissive in some areas, and permissive states can seem rigid. Some states require that the home school teacher be certified or request that certain types of curriculum be followed.

Many changes have been made in recent years, mainly because of the growing number of people choosing this alternative. In one year alone, seven states enacted new laws concerning home education, and in three other states, there were court cases that effectively canceled previous restrictions on home schools.

COMPULSORY ATTENDANCE

There is no one general overview of state laws concerning the home school alternative, except to note that all 50 states have compulsory attendance laws. Most of these laws require children to attend school between the ages of 7 and 16, although there is some variance here. Some states require school entrance as early as age 5, or as late as age 8. Sometimes the maximum age for leaving school is 14, while some states require attendance beyond age 16.

HOME SCHOOLS: An Alternative

COMPETING INTERESTS

The reasons behind compulsory attendance laws may be found by studying the history of American public education (Chapter 7). But the issue today boils down to the competing interests of the family versus the state. Parents choosing to educate their young at home have a vested interest in doing so: the welfare of their own children. The states also have an interest in the welfare of children in general, and have the power to legislate their concerns into law. States have a financial interest in keeping each child in public schools, for the sake of gaining federal funds. The state's interests are not always unselfish, but generally it can make it seem so.

Whose rights should prevail? Even the Supreme Court, in *Yoder vs. Wisconsin,* 1972, recognized the conflicts:

> *A State's interest in universal education, however highly we rank it, is not totally free from a balancing process when it infringes on fundamental rights and interests.*

States have gone beyond the simple age requirements of compulsory attendance laws. Besides requiring that children be educated, they have directed how, where, and by whom. These are the issues that cause conflict between the schools and concerned parents.

Home schoolers have no quarrel that children should be educated. All parents want their children to learn about the world around them. Parents choosing home instruction have no argument with the state's desire for children to learn; parents object to the conditions that the state requires beyond that, especially when the state excludes parental freedom of choice. As one home schooling parent said, "We're willing to cooperate. We all feel that every child should be required to have an education, but it's hardly fair that we have only one choice."

CONSTITUTIONALITY

Home schoolers have been challenging the compulsory attendance laws on the basis of constitutionality and parental sovereignty, pleading parents' right to choose the type of schooling their children receive. Step by step, in court rulings, they have gained a foothold on the rights they never should have been denied.

Years ago, the foundation for home schools was laid in the courts. In 1893, *Commonwealth vs. Roberts,* it was decided that "the great object of the [compulsory attendance] provision of the statutes has been that children be educated, not that they be educated in any particular way." Although it did not specifically mention home schools, it did concede to parental freedom of choice.

Choosing an alternative type of schooling was protected in 1925 by *Pierce vs. Society of Sisters:*

> *The fundamental theory of liberty upon which all governments in this Union repose excludes any general power of the state to standardize its children by forcing them to accept instruction from public teachers only. The child is not the mere creature of the state; those who nurture him and direct his destiny have the right, coupled with the high duty, to recognize and prepare him for additional obligations.*

The wording of the Pierce ruling indicates quite clearly that freedom of choice is not only a parent's right, but also his responsibility, a duty not to be carried lightly. It allowed parents to choose private schools over public schools.

Recent rulings have upheld the constitutionality of home schooling for religious reasons, *Wisconsin vs. Yoder,* 1972, and for constitutional guarantees "in addition to those contained in the First Amendments," *Perchemlides vs. Frizzle,* 1978.

Yoder was a Wisconsin Amish parent who was granted First Amendment protection for home schooling on the basis of his religion. His attachment to his convictions appeared to be an important part of the ruling. This instituted the *conviction vs. preference* issue (more in Chapter 4).

Further rulings showed that parents need not adhere to any specific religious beliefs in order to choose alternative schooling. This widens the parent's prerogative.

One recent constitutional battle concerning home schools was the 1978 Massachusetts case of Perchemlides. The state superior court upheld the Perchemlides family's decision to home school, declaring there is a constitutional statutory protection of the right to home education.

Several other decisions on the constitutionality of home schools in regard to the competing interests of the family versus the state have also upheld the family's right to choose the type of education their children receive. In *Vermont vs. LeBarge,* 1976, *Minnesota vs. Lundsten,* 1980, and several others, the courts have determined that compulsory attendance laws must yield to First Amendment rights and other constitutional restraints.

> ## SIMPLY SAID, PARENTS HAVE THE CONSTITUTIONAL RIGHT TO HOME SCHOOL!!

EQUIVALENCY BATTLE

Although the parents' constitutional rights have been upheld by the courts, the states still have had an ace up their sleeves. They still have the regulatory power to set educational standards for school-age children. This is called the "equivalency battle," or the states' imposition of its educational standards on home schools. Technically, home schools are allowed as long as they provide an "equivalent instruction."

Courts have generally enforced the states' right to set and regulate its educational standards, within reason. However, it has been explained that they may not set standards so stringent that private schools and home schools are prevented from carrying out their purposes [*Farrington vs. Tokushique,* 1927].

A similar decision was in *Ohio vs. Wisner,* 1976, where the state's minimum standards were described as:

So pervasive and all-encompassing that total

*compliance with each and every standard by a
non-public school would effectively eradicate the
distinction between public and non-public education, and thereby deprive these appellants of their
traditional interest as parents to direct the up-
bringing and education of their children.*

In other words, the state can expect home schoolers to meet certain
criteria, but those criteria must not be punitively defined. The state cannot expect
home schoolers to conform to irrationally high expectations.

The equivalency battle has been the grounds on which most home
schoolers have been harassed recently. State requirements have often violated the
guidelines as set up by the court rulings, and have been so rigidly impossible that
many parents can't meet all of them.

Educators such as Allen Gunderson, chairman of the Montana Board of
Education, want legislation passed that is tough on home schoolers. Gunderson
would like home schoolers to be required to demonstrate that they are complying with
certain criteria, such as 180 days of pupil instruction, certification of the school's
administrator [parent], and keeping records of attendance and measures of achievement. Thus the parent who is genuinely concerned with the welfare of his own
children would become bogged down with mountains of red tape and bureaucratic
forms.

Some states have been moving toward tough laws for parents to prove
equivalency. But the courts have offered home schoolers some protection. In the
Perchemlides ruling, the state had the burden of proof to show beyond a reasonable
doubt that the parents had not established equivalency. The court believed equivalency did not need to be a carbon copy of the public school's curriculum.

The important legal decision here was that the state had the burden of
proof, not the parents. In other words, the parents are assumed competent until the
state proves otherwise.

The implications are that states may not deprive parents of their constitutional right to choose home schooling unless the parents are seriously neglecting the
education of their children. South Dakota is one state that has a policy reflecting this

---

attitude. Superintendents are advised to accept all home school plans unless there is significant reason to doubt the sincerity of the parent's home school proposal, such as evidence that the parents are keeping their children out of school to work. This resolution of the competing interests of the parents versus the state is significant.

In the Perchemlides case, Judge Greany stated:

> *There are certain ways in which individualized home instruction can never be "equivalent" of any in-school education, public or private. At home, there are no other students, no classrooms, no pre-existing schedules. The parents stand in a very different relationship to their children than do teachers in a class full of other people's children. In view of these differences, to require congruent "equivalency" is self-defeating because it might foreclose the use of teaching methods less formalized, but in the home more effective than those used in the classroom. For example, certain step-by-step programs of graded instruction, involving the use of standardized texts and tests periodically administered, might be unnecessary when the parent-teacher enjoys a constant communication with the child, and so is able to monitor his or her comprehension and progress on an individualized level impossible in school.*

The judge showed his perceptiveness about the inherent problems in public education, and the inherent advantages of home instruction. He also clearly stated that a one-to-one equivalency need not be demanded from home schoolers. For instance, a home school plan need not use exactly the same textbooks, or phrase its curriculum as "Science I leading to Science II."

The ruling also supports a previous decision of *New Jersey vs. Massa,* 1967, which declared that a home instruction plan may not be rejected on the grounds that the social environment differs from the classroom. In the social context, "different" for the home schools means "better." Equivalency of the education itself was the only criteria allowed to be compared in that ruling.

TEACHER CERTIFICATION

The toughest litigation parents have faced concerns teacher certification. Some states still require that home schoolers be certified teachers in order to meet their equivalency standards. Although many home schoolers are indeed certified, the vast majority of them are not. Legal battles are continuing to wage over this distinction.

A landmark ruling, *Michigan vs. Nobel,* 1979, exempted Ruth Nobel from the teaching certification requirement based on her religious convictions against certification. Expert testimony was given to show that teacher certification does not necessarily produce teacher competence. Professor Donald Erickson of the University of San Francisco declared that there has been no empirical evidence to support the contention that a teaching certificate yields a superior education for the students. Students taught by uncertified teachers, such as those in certain private schools, score better on standardized test than their public school counterparts.

Many of the home schoolers who have won their court cases were not certified teachers, and equivalency was decided on different criteria.

A newsworthy case concerning equivalency and certification has been the Sessions' battle in Iowa. They have been prosecuted three times in that state, with favorable decisions the first two times.

The court ruled that the state had not proved that the family had not provided instruction that was equivalent to instruction by a certified teacher elsewhere. The school board prosecuted again, saying it "had no problem with the quality of the education the children were getting, and that the program was equivalent; for them the only issue is the technicality of how much time per week the children must spend with a certified teacher."

The Decorah, Iowa, school board was obviously less concerned about the welfare of the children than about a minor technicality. Indeed, they admitted that the children were receiving an adequate education. It's at this point that the state should yield to the parents in the battle of competing interests.

Home schoolers need the support of legislators, judges, and educators. When this issue has been legally proven once and for all in all of the states, then the legal pathway will be very welcoming for home schools.

THE BUDKE STORY

The Budkes were taken to court three times in a battle over Minnesota's ambiguous statutes.

Donald and Kathleen Budke are the parents of 13 children; the oldest is 37 years old. The older children attended public schools, but over the years these parents noticed in the schools a "gradual deterioration in the morals, values, disciplines, the whole picture."

Years ago they decided to withdraw three of the younger children, then ages 7, 10, and 11, from public schools. They cited religious reasons as their primary motive, but also felt that there were academic, social, financial, moral, and psychological implications:

> At the time we removed our children from the public schools, our fifth-grader was a very poor reader. He was also poor in spelling. Our second grader had undergone a personality change which was very negative. The double standard in the moral atmosphere on the school bus and in school [as compared to home] was very confusing for the child.

The Budkes found that the values promoted at school were very different from their own convictions, which they had been trying very hard to instill in their children.

> The (sometimes subtle and sometimes blatant) promotion of Secular Humanist tenets, the Secular Humanist philosophy that is forced on children in the public school system is directly opposed to our Christian beliefs. Parental sovereignty is ques-

tioned and ridiculed. The child is taught that there are no absolutes. Everything is situational. Christian beliefs are questioned and ridiculed. The whole educational system is built on the premise that "There is no God. You are on your own."

After withdrawing the children from public schools, Kathleen began teaching them at home, using materials from the Christian Liberty Academy. Later, they switched to picking their own textbooks, using as a guide the curriculum of Our Lady of Victory School, a traditional Catholic school in California.

The reaction of friends and relatives to Budkes' home schooling decision was decidedly mixed; however, other people's response was usually favorable. Three public school teachers personally called to express support.

Academically and socially, the children developed well. Each year they were given standardized tests in a nearby parochial school, and were progressing more than a grade level each year. Kathleen has been pleased with the children's social development, which has been more natural than the stilted development that takes place at school due to peer pressure. The children are able to socialize well with all ages instead of being categorized into certain groups.

In spite of their pure motives, and in spite of the fact that the children were advancing more than adequately, the Budkes were prosecuted three times in five years for violation of Minnesota's compulsory attendance laws.

The first case was decided in the Otter Tail County Court by Judge Sigwel Wood. Several competent witnesses were produced to defend the Budkes. John Marlett, a former teacher and school superintendent, testified that he had observed Kathleen's teaching methods and that she was very well qualified to teach her children. He approved of her preparation, the materials used, and the classroom standards that were maintained.

A local priest, Father Richard Stineman, testified that Kathleen had been a teacher in the local Catholic CCD program, and that the couple's religious convictions were sincere.

John Eidsmoe of Oral Roberts University in Tulsa, Oklahoma, and attorney for the Budkes, pleaded their case on constitutional grounds that they be exempted from compulsory attendance laws because it violated their freedom of religion. The First and Fourteenth Amendments were pleaded. He also argued that Kathleen Budke was a competent teacher and that his clients should not be found guilty solely on that ground.

Nonetheless, Judge Wood ruled that the Budkes were in violation of the law because Kathleen was not a certified teacher, and he believed that she did not meet the state requirements that children be "taught by teachers who are essentially equivalent to the minimum standards for public school teachers of the same grades or subjects." To him, "essentially equivalent" meant certified, and he ruled against the family.

The Budkes appealed to the District Court, where three judges unanimously ruled in their favor, stating that Minnesota's statute 120.10 was unconstitutional when applied to the Budkes because it violated rights stipulated in the First and Fourteenth Amendments. However, the state was not ready to admit defeat, and the Minnesota Attorney General appealed to the Minnesota Supreme Court.

On July 19, 1985, the Minnesota Supreme Court unanimously ruled that Minnesota's compulsory attendance law was unconstitutional because of vagueness and therefore was violating the family's right to due process under the Fourteenth Amendment. The court believed that it was unnecessary to address the First Amendment issue that had been raised in the case.

The Budkes are only one of many families who have been in the judicial process for following their convictions. Most families who have been through the judicial process eventually win favorable rulings. We applaud these families for having the strength and fortitude to endure these lengthy court proceedings, for in doing so they are paving the way for other families to provide the best possible education and family environment for their children.

COURT CASES PYRAMID

The court cases pyramid shows the number of litigations concerning home schools. The bottom layer is the numerous judicial decisions over the past 100 years concerning compulsory attendance laws that have been in defense of parental

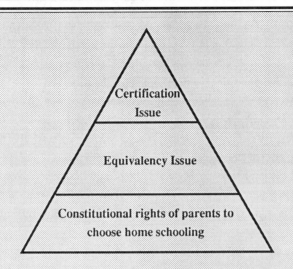

COURT CASES PYRAMID
Number of home schooler litigations
This shows that groundwork of the legal issues has been done. Now there may be "fine-tuning" in the way states perceive their position to regulate homeschoolers.

sovereignty and the freedom of choice in education, the basic constitutional issue.

The middle layer shows that a smaller number of decisions have been made concerning the issue of equivalency of instruction, which plagues some home schoolers today.

The top and smallest layer is the rulings about the constitutionality of requiring certification of home schoolers. This may be the stickiest issue of all.

Because of the depth and breadth of the many court cases involving the basic constitutional issues of compulsory schooling, the bottom layer is securely entrenched in the minds of the courts. Any well-prepared case today should have little problem defending the constitutional rights of parental choice in education.

However, the middle layer is in less-tested waters. Legislators in many states have been trying to clarify by law this undefined area. Home schoolers must be well-informed about the bills that are introduced in their state, so that a lobby can be organized either in support of or in opposition to the legislation. Statewide appeals by home schoolers in Wisconsin may have been part of the reason legislation was passed in that state protecting the rights of home schoolers.

Much of the ambiguity about certification has been clarified in many states. However, until certification requirements are ruled unconstitutional in no uncertain terms, and not just on religious grounds, there is a great deal of work to be done. Courageous parents are battling the issue in many states.

The Home School Legal Defense Association has been actively challenging certification requirements in several states over the years. It also has initiated civil rights actions in states where vagueness of the law has resulted in litigation against parents.

Clarification of these issues is necessary, either through judicial review or through legislation. Wherever ambiguity of the law still exists, it still needs changing, so that home schoolers know exactly where they stand legally.

LEGAL DEVELOPMENTS CONCERNING PARENT'S FREEDOM OF CHOICE CAN BE STUDIED BY READING:

Legal Limits of Authority Over the Pupil. **Edward C Bolmeier. Charlottesville, VA: The Michie Company.**

Education by Choice: The Case for Family Control. **John E. Coons & Stephan D. Sugarman. Los Angeles, CA: University of CA Press.**

The Courts and the Public Schools. **Newton Edwards. Chicago, IL: University of Chicago Press.**

<u>**IMPORTANT ADDRESSES:**</u>

HSDLA—Home School Legal Defense Association, PO Box 159, Paeonian Springs VA 21219. (703) 882-3838. Available is a quarterly newsletter for $20 a year. This association is actively involved with home school legal cases in many states, and is active in challenging the laws where necessary.

NALSAS—National Association for the Legal Support of Alternative Schools, Ed Nagel, director. PO Box 2823, Santa Fe NM 87504-2823.

CHAPTER NINE
State Laws & Home Schoolers

Families will have to choose the legal path they will follow. A parent considering home education should become acquainted with applicable laws and court decisions, especially those affecting his state. The local support group has undoubtedly already researched it. No matter what option the family picks, a support group can offer advice, moral support, and even give ideas on teaching. They will be well aware of the legal trends, the legal climate in that particular state, and will know where to turn for legal information. They may even know of attorneys, superintendents, and legislators friendly to their cause.

Also very useful is a subscription to the newsletter and legal maps supplied by the Home School Legal Defense Association (address at the end of this chapter).

An excellent description of the laws in each state is provided in *Home School: Taking the First Step* by Borg Hendrickson. This book also provides the major forms that might be needed to cooperate with state laws, such as lesson plans, immunization records, and other record-keeping.

After a family is well versed in the laws of their state, there are several paths from which to choose.

HOME SCHOOLS: An Alternative

OPTIONS

1. Cooperate with school authorities.

According to Gustavsen's study, 62% of the home schoolers he surveyed were operating with the approval of the local school authorities. Half of these said that they had obtained formal approval; the other half said it was informal approval.

Realize what formal approval may entail. In some states, the home schoolers must be certified teachers. In other states, an approved curriculum must be followed. Also, the children might be required to be tested every year, and usually approval must be sought again each year.

These conditions are the reasons many home schoolers have had legal battles. The certification requirement is often enough grounds for superintendents to begin prosecution. Other times, they do not give approval of the curriculum unless it is identical to what the public schools are providing.

Families seeking to cooperate with school authorities should be aware of whether or not they can expect cooperation in return. Local support groups can often supply this information, plus give ideas of what types of home school plans are most likely to be accepted in that area. But it is still up to the discretion of that authority to say "Ay" or "Nay" on an individual basis.

The attitude that a parent has as he approaches the school authority is also very important. The attitude should be friendly, not critical. Even if the parent feels very strongly that the schools are a bad influence on his children, he should keep these opinions to himself when discussing home schooling with local authorities. If the parent extends an attitude of cooperation, he is more likely to receive that same attitude in return. School authorities are people, and tend to react negatively to harsh criticism. And you really can't blame them, so why start the fire?

A cooperative attitude will go a long way if you ever need help from local school authorities, such as advice in locating a tutor for difficult subjects, or if you ever want your children to return to the public schools. It would be unwise to ever burn the bridges.

Also keep in mind the special pressures that might be on the administrators and teachers. They are required to submit a lot of bureaucratic forms to the state, and everything they do is analyzed and recorded. Therefore, if they ask for you to fill our special forms, it might be because they are required to give them to the state. If you happen to object to some of the documentation required, do so in as friendly a way as possible, and find out whether it is a state requirement, or their own special design. From this information you can decide whether your objections will cause legal problems or whether the documentation can actually be avoided.

2. Incorporate as a private school.

Many times the wisest legal path is to incorporate as a private school. In some states, parents who follow this option are not harassed if they strictly follow the state's guidelines for private schools. In Kansas, the attorney for the Kansas State Department of Education said, "If they register as a private school, then the presumption is that they're a private school, and they're within the law."

Yet this doesn't always work. Tom and Bonnie Sawyer of Spring Hill, Kansas, established a private school to educate their children, but they were prosecuted because authorities didn't believe that Bonnie was a "competent" teacher.

An advantage of incorporating as a private school is that many states do not have strict regulations over these schools. Usually private school teachers do not need to be certified (except in North Dakota, where you can't do anything, it seems.) Private schools do not have to follow a set curriculum. Sometimes the state requires attendance records, and some states require various other records.

Another interesting point about using private school laws for home schools is that some statutes are more liberal for private schools than they are for tutors, which is a classification that would probably include most home schoolers. Private schools in some states are not regulated, but tutors are.

Another reason that parents incorporate as private schools is because the home schooling laws in that state may not be applied fairly and judicially. Laws may exist on the books that look ideal, but in application they have been known to be abusive and unfair. In these states, home schools have often turned to the option of incorporating as a private school.

3. Enroll in a correspondence school.

Many parents are nervous at first about starting a home school. They are unsure about how to develop a curriculum and frightened at the thought of being prosecuted. These parents often enroll their children in correspondence schools, of which there are many. A few are listed at the end of Chapter 12. Legal threats sometimes stop when parent notify authorities that their children are enrolled in "XYZ School."

4. Establish a satellite school.

Parents who want to develop their own curriculum but still have their children "enrolled" somewhere to avoid legal problems sometimes become a satellite school to an already established organization. Other parents form satellites of private schools established by other home schoolers. In Virginia, local parents had satellite schools of Brook School, the private school of the Geisy family. In reality, all the families were home schooling, but felt that they had legal protection by their association with a legal private school.

5. Keep a low profile.

This option is what some parents have chosen. They have simply withdrawn their children from school or never enrolled them in the first place. It's easiest if the children have never been enrolled in school. They don't advertise what they have done, but they feel it's the only way they can choose the alternative they want.

In states where the legal climate has traditionally not been friendly to home schooling, this option is very popular. A leader of a Michigan support group years ago told me that most of the home schoolers in that state are keeping a low profile because school districts have had a "search and destroy" attitude. He advises parents against writing to the State Department of Education because these letters have been followed back to the families. Even a simple request for information has lead to threats about keeping the kids in school.

STATE LAWS

The trouble with categorizing state laws is that the written statutes are often ambiguous and the way states apply them is a category in itself. Also, state laws concerning home schools are changing every month. The best bet for current information on state laws is to contact the Home School Legal Defense Association (address at the end of the chapter) and get a subscription to their newsletter and legal maps. Also, *The Home School Manual* is frequently updated with extensive legal information for each state (address at the end of the chapter). And *Home School: Taking the First Step* contains an excellent summary of the laws of each state.

The map included in this chapter is designed to give an idea of the general legal climate of each state, and whether it's been generally friendly or unfriendly to home schoolers.

The ratings for the map mean:

1. Ideal states for home schooling.
   These states do not require certification of home school teachers. Their home school laws are clear and unambiguous. Home schools have been treated fairly in these states.

2. States where home schoolers have generally been treated well.
   These states may have vague laws, but do not usually provoke litigation. Some of the states, such as South Dakota and Louisiana, require approval of a home school, but this approval is easily gained. None of these states require that a home school teacher be certified.

3. States that have fairly numerous regulations and/or some strict regulations.
   Most states fit this category. These states do not specifically require certification

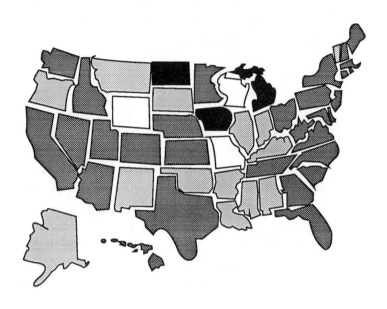

LEGAL CLIMATE FOR HOME SCHOOLS

☐ 1. Ideal states for home schooling.

▨ 2. States where home schoolers have generally been treated well.

▨ 3. States that have numerous and/or some strict regulations regarding home schooling.

■ 4. States that are very very strict regarding home school regulations.

of home school teachers, but may require "equivalency" of curriculum and approval of local authorities. Herein lies the possible conflict. Local authorities who have the right of approval may interpret "equivalency" to mean that the teacher must be certified. Other times they may require certain curriculum or certain guidelines be followed.

4. States with strict regulations and an unfavorable legal climate for home schoolers. These states may require certification, and have extensive time-consuming requirements, such as certain record-keeping or state-required subjects. North Dakota has always been a difficult state for home schooling. The following example shows how mean-spirited North Dakota has been in the past. Hopefully, we will not see any future examples like this.

THE NORTH DAKOTA SPELLING BEE

Cara Transtrom, age 14, was denied the chance to compete in the 1989 McKenzie County's Spelling Bee. Why? She won the county spelling bee the prior year and went on to place second in the state. So what's the problem? Well, you see, she is a home schooled student who is taught by her parents, who don't happen to be certified teachers. In North Dakota, all home schooled students must be taught by a certified teacher, which puts her parents in violation of the state law.

Not only that, but the school district was embarrassed by a home schooled student spelling better than publicly schooled children. So the next year the county superintendent wrote a new rule, stating that all competitors must be from a public or accredited private school. That meant Cara couldn't compete.

It was a very mean-spirited way to eliminate competition for the public schoolchildren, and also a way to harass home schoolers. But lucky for Cara, the state school superintendent stepped in, and said Cara could compete. But it still shows just how far certain districts or certain authorities will go to make trouble for home schoolers who are successfully educating their children.

HOME SCHOOLS: An Alternative

SUMMARY

All of the states plus the District of Columbia permit home schools in one form or another. But just because a state "allows" home schools doesn't mean that it's easy to be a home schooler in that state. However, with the help of a support group, parents have found that the legal groundwork for homeschooling isn't as difficult as they anticipated. Homeschooling parents will tell you it's definitely worth the effort!

CURRENT LEGAL INFORMATION IS AVAILABLE FROM:

HSDLA—Home School Legal Defense Association, PO Box 159, Paeonian Springs VA 22129. (703) 882-3838. A year's subscription to a legal information map is $20. This map is updated every three months. Also available is a quarterly newsletter for $20 a year. This association is actively involved with home school legal cases in many states, and is active in challenging the laws where necessary.

NALSAS—National Association for the Legal Support of Alternative Schools, Ed Nagel, director. PO Box 2823, Santa Fe NM 87504-2823. (Previous address; was not able to find this organization recently.)

Growing Without Schooling, Holt Associates, 2269 Massachusetts Ave., Cambridge MA 02140. (617) 864-3100. This national bimonthly home schooling newsletter contains legal updates each issue.

The Home School Manual, by Ted Wade, 6th edition, $24.95. Gazelle Publications, 9853 Jericho Road, Bridgman MI 49106.

Home School: Taking the First Step, revised edition by Borg Hendrickson, $16.95. Mountain Meadow Press, PO Box 447, Kooskia ID 83539. (208) 926-7875. This book has a summary of homeschooling laws for each state.

CHAPTER TEN
Frequently Asked Questions About Homeschooling

1. Why do people choose homeschooling?

Traditionally, most people were choosing homeschooling for religious reasons, but that has been changing. In 1985, 75% of the people choosing homeschooling were doing so for religious reasons. In 1996, that rate is about 50%, with the other 50% mainly choosing it as a reaction against public schools. The people who are choosing it because they dislike the public schools are the fastest growing segment of the homeschool population.

2. What do people object to about public schools?

Parents dislike the preponderance of guns, drugs, and violence in schools. They are sending their kids to school to be educated, not to be the victims of violence and drug activity.

Every day, as I do radio shows and talk to people around the nation about homeschooling, I hear horror stories about what's happening—and what is failing to happen—in the public schools. What is *happening* is that well-behaved children go to school, and they return with bad language, bad behavior, and bad attitudes. Negative peer pressure is a terrible problem within the schools. What is *failing to happen* is academics. The schools are failing many kids in providing a basic education. Today a woman called to complain that her granddaughter, a fifth grader, could not read at all, so they are going to start to homeschool her.

3. How many people have chosen homeschooling in the United States?

The growth of homeschooling in the United States has been phenomenal. In 1980, there were only 25,000 homeschoolers, in 1985, about 50,000, and by 1996, there are 1,200,000. The growth rate is 25% per year, which means that by the year 2000, there will be 2,000,000 homeschoolers.

Some local support groups are reporting as much as 500% annual growth. The concept of homeschooling is becoming a mainstream movement!

4. Is it legal to homeschool?

It is legal to homeschool in all 50 states and the District of Columbia. However, each state varies in its laws regarding how homeschooling is regulated. There are states where it is very easy to homeschool, and a few states where it is very difficult, but most states fall in the middle, with some requirements concerning enrollment, curriculum, record-keeping or standardized tests.

5. How can these kids become socialized if they are not in school?

Homeschooled kids are not isolated. They can socialize with other children after school, and during activities in the community. These children participate in a wide variety of socializing activities such as church events, community activities, clubs such as Boy Scouts, Girl Scouts, YMCA, and so forth. Many homeschool support groups provide events for the children. A Fountain Hills, Arizona, group holds a weekly science project for the homeschooled children, as well as regular field trips.

What is interesting about homeschooled children is that they learn to socialize with people of all ages, not just with children their own age. In doing so, they are able to avoid peer pressure that is so often a negative influence on young people.

6. What are the benefits to the children from homeschooling?

Children benefit from homeschooling academically, socially, and emotionally. One of the greatest benefits to both parent and child is the emotional bonding that takes place during homeschooling. Children who are sent to school at a young age are deprived of completing the bonding process that has started to take place between them and their parents. Homeschooled children develop a strong identity and sense of self worth, so that even if they return to school at a later date, they are able to deflect negative peer pressure.

One gentleman who called in on one of my radio shows knew several homeschooled children. He said that they were "all-American kids," the kind you'd be proud to have as your child or as your friend. I agree.

The best evidence that homeschooling works is the *children*!

Academically, homeschooled children generally test 2-3 grade levels above their peers. There are many homeschool success stories, as shown in Chapter 6.

7. Do children enjoy homeschooling-are they content being educated this way?

The general consensus is that the children appreciate being homeschooled. I asked my daughter, Sarah, who was homeschooled from the age of 8 until she started college at 15, to answer this question, and she said, "Whenever people ask me if I enjoyed homeschooling, I tell them it supplied me extra opportunities that would not have been available in the schools, and it provided me with a strong bond to my parents." She said that people tended to agree that's what they had heard from other homeschoolers.

8. Can homeschooled children enter college?

Yes. The colleges differ in their admissions requirements, and the children must fill those requirements. But when filling out an application, put "Home Schooled" or "Diploma from XYZ Correspondence School (whichever used)" on the line that asks for high school information.

My daughter started community college at 15, and did not need to take any SAT or ACT to enroll. The dean of the school did ask to interview her because they interview all early graduating high school students who wish to enroll. He simply asked her if she really wanted to do it, and if she felt she could handle it. She said, yes, yes, and was enrolled. Later, she graduated from community college and was automatically accepted at the university level. No entrance exam was ever necessary. This is probably the exception, not the rule. Probably most homeschooled students will be required to take an entrance exam at some point.

Most colleges are welcoming homeschooled students because they are excellent students and eager to continue their learning experience. Check with the college of your choice and find out what admissions requirements are for homeschooled students.

9. How do educators feel about homeschooling?

Generally, they have either a positive attitude or an open mind about homeschooling. Some wonder if parents have enough background to teach their own kids, especially upper level things like chemistry, physics, calculus, etc. In reply to that, I tell them that parents are free to seek outside help (correspondence courses, fully designed curriculums, friends, relatives, homeschool support groups) for courses that are challenging. Other than that, it does not take a teaching degree to pass on knowledge.

One interesting note about educators and homeschooling is that many professional educators themselves are turning to homeschooling for their own children. That's a very strong indictment on the condition of public education.

10. Where does a parent find homeschool materials?

A good starting point for finding materials is to join the local support group. Some of these groups have a library of materials that can be checked out. Also, many groups are conducting statewide conventions and curriculum fairs. In Arizona, for instance, the Arizona Families for Home Education hold an annual Convention and Curriculum Fair for two days in either May or June. This gives parents a chance to review materials by exhibitors, listen to speakers, and visit workshops.

An obvious and inexpensive choice for finding materials is the library. Some materials, especially for lower grades, can easily be found in supermarkets and larger pharmacies.

For more resources, check the *Home Education Resource Guide*, a book by Blue Bird Publishing. Order form is at the end of this book.

11. How does a parent find the time to homeschool their children? What if both parents work full-time?

Basically, if there is a commitment, parents will find the time. One teacher spends her days in the public schools, and homeschools her children in the evenings and on weekends. That's dedication!

For most people it would be difficult to work fulltime and be dedicated to homeschooling. Therefore, it usually takes one parent to be in the home—at least half days—to homeschool. This may cause a pinch financially, but if the children are truly a priority, the adjustment can be made. Many times parents are finding that a home office or a home business is the perfect solution. That way, they can work in the home and still be available to homeschool the children.

12. Can a homeschooled child reenter school?

Yes, it's generally quite easy for homeschooled children to reenter public school. There may be some requirements by the school, such as a standardized test. That is no problem, because most homeschooled children score very well on these exams. Any records kept by the parent, especially those required by the state, may be examined by the school, so that's when records come in particularly handy.

13. How does a parent start, if they are interested in homeschooling?

The first step is to join a homeschool support group. The group will give parents confidence to start the process, can prepare them for the legal qualifications in their area, and show them where to obtain materials. The support group contains both parents and children, so new members can see how well adjusted the homeschool kids are! The main ingredient is commitment. So get started!

CHAPTER ELEVEN
Teachers are People Too!

I took a national survey of professional educators about home schooling and this chapter is about the results of that survey. I wanted them to have the chance to voice their opinions.

SURVEY PROCEDURES

A sample of 200 educators was chosen from among all of the public schools in the United States. They were chosen because those particular districts were known to have home schools operating within them. It was important for the respondents to have a working knowledge of home schools in order for them to have an opinion about them. However, the selection was not made on a pre-determined basis of those school districts' attitudes. I did not know in advance whether any particular school district was friendly or unfriendly to home schoolers. This selection basis was important to keep the responses objective.

The names of home schooling families were kept confidential; I made no references ever to a particular person or family in any school district.

Each socio-economic and geographic area of the continental United States was represented. There were school districts in the North, South, East, West, and Midwest. Schools represented urban and rural areas.

The questionnaire contained six multiple choice questions, designed for simplicity and for statistical analysis. Another question asked for any further comments on the subject. Two questions asked for more local information for home school research. The name/school/city/state/grade level or administrative position was on each form.

The questionnaire was pre-tested on two schools in Michigan, with 100% reply, and no suggested alterations.

Of the 200 questionnaires, 115 were returned completed. Fourteen others were returned unanswered. Three respondents said they did not wish to participate in the survey; one of them did not like the format of the questionnaire. One completed form had to be disqualified from statistical analysis because the respondent made the note that he didn't know anything about home schools, which defeats the purpose of an opinion survey.

Of the respondents:

> *59% were rural and 41% were urban;*
> *48% were teachers and 52% were administrators.*

When significant statistical differences occurred between either of these categories, it it noted directly below the response.

QUESTION #1: AS A PROFESSIONAL EDUCA-TOR, I FEEL THAT A HOME EDUCATION IS:

Total Response

10%	Always detrimental to children.
	[All responses here from rural.]
90%	Sometimes beneficial to children, depending on the factors involved.
0%	Always beneficial to children.

Chapter Eleven: Teachers are People Too!

HOME SCHOOLS: An Alternative

This question was designed as a general attitude indicator. The responses given in later questions can be compared to this first question to see if there is a consistency in the answers. There did seem to be a consistency, since the respondents who were negative on this first question also replied with negative attitudes later on.

Most of the respondents were ambivalent about home schools, with an attitude of "Let's judge each case on its own merits." This general attitude seemed to prevail throughout the survey.

QUESTION #2: THE FACTORS THAT DECIDE THE SUCCESS OF A HOME EDUCATION ARE:

(check as many as apply)

Total   Response

59%   Education level of parents

83%   Motivation of parents
        [Urban 67%, rural 88%]

66%   Motivation of child
        [Urban 58%, rural 71%]
        [Administrators 53%, teachers 79%]

76%   Reasons that parents decided to educate their children at home
        [Urban 92%, rural 65%]
        [Administrators 67%, teachers 86%]

10%   Occupation of parents

3%   Income of parents

66%   Preparation of curriculum by parents
        [Urban 75%, rural 59%]
        [Administrators 73%, teachers 57%]

41%   Other (specify)

Numbers add to more than 100% because more than one response could be checked.

Comments for "Other" included: cooperation with local officials; consistency of instruction; attitude concerning society in general; teaching skills of parents; relationship between parent and child; and the ability of the child to work independently.

An interesting observation is that administrators place a greater importance on curriculum than do teachers. It could be that teachers are closer to classroom experience and know that curriculum is not the most important part of learning.

QUESTION #3: REASONS THAT PARENTS MIGHT DECIDE TO EDUCATE THEIR CHILDREN AT HOME MIGHT BE:

(check as many as apply)

Total	Response
66%	It fits their lifestyle
86%	Religion
79%	The parents do not believe that the public schools are providing an adequate education. [Urban 83%, rural 71%]
62%	The parents are afraid of the drugs, violence, and other problems that their children might be exposed to through the public schools. {urban 65%, rural 53%]
17%	The parents are social misfits.
48%	Other (specify)

Numbers add to more than 100% because more than one response could be checked.

HOME SCHOOLS: An Alternative

"Other" included: racial (urban response); a different philosophy of education; personal philosophy of child-rearing; kids dislike of schools; family may be traveling.

This question tried to measure how well educators understood the reasons that parents choose home education. The replies correlate well with the types of answers parents would have given themselves: religion; academic; lifestyle; and social problems (drugs, violence) in schools. A few educators felt that parents choosing this alternative must be socially maladjusted. That doesn't click with findings by Gustavsen, Holt, Moore and myself that show home schoolers to be conservative and socially well adjusted.

> QUESTION #4: WOULD YOU, AS A PROFESSIONAL EDUCATOR, COOPERATE WITH PARENTS WHO HAD CHOSEN HOME SCHOOLING FOR THEIR CHILDREN?
>
> Total   Response
>
> 93%   Yes
> 7%   No [All responses here from rural]

Again, this is a general attitude indicator, as a check for the answers to question number 1. The answers are similar. All of the "No" replies were again rural, with slightly more people willing to help home schoolers even though they checked a negative response for question number 1. Notes on the side gave a clue why: Some of the educators said they would help a home schooler if the child was ill or had special needs, but for no other reason.

The overwhelming positive response to this question by both teachers and administrators surprised me. This attitude is refreshing and encouraging. It seems to indicate that if home schoolers approach the schools with a positive and cooperative attitude when they decide to home school, they are more likely to receive a positive attitude and cooperation in return.

QUESTION #5: THE DISADVANTAGES OF HOME SCHOOLING ARE:
(check as many as apply)

<u>Total</u> <u>Response</u>

55% Lack of monitoring of the child's academic progress.
   [Urban 83%, rural 35%]

83% Lack of social development in the child.

59% Lack of competition in the child's academic and social worlds.
   [Urban 83%, rural 41%]

79% Lack of the type of stimulation of ideas provided by the classroom.
   [Urban 92%, rural 71%]

38% Lack of qualified instructors.
   [Administrators 67%, teachers 29%]

48% Lack of facilities.
   [Administrators 67%, teachers 29%]

24% Other (specify)

Numbers add to more than 100% because more than one response could be checked.

HOME SCHOOLS: An Alternative

Some "Other" answers were: it's a form of elitism; the child feels different; the parents have a negative attitude towards education; the child learns to deal with only one type of authority figure; tendency of parent to impose his will on the child; no way to insure properly balanced curriculum; and lack of acceptance of this type of education by society.

The question was designed by listing the objections that educators had to home schools throughout my research. The purpose was to determine how strong these various objections really are.

Their main objection was the belief that social development of the home schooled child would be hindered. This idea has been explored thoroughly in Chapter 3, and parents have found that the social development of the home schooled children is much more natural than that of their publicly schooled counterparts.

The second major objection was the lack of idea stimulation. That myth was covered in Chapter 5. Modern education tends to strangle the growth of ideas rather than to stimulate them. Ideas are a part of the spontaneous nature of learning, but that type of learning is not encouraged in schools.

Interestingly, administrators have a much greater faith in the necessity of public school facilities than do the teachers. That's possibly because administrators are a couple of steps removed from the realities of the classroom. Another explanation could be that they have faith in their facilities because they are in charge of the budget. Perhaps teachers have a more realistic view of school facilities.

One objection that an educator listed was quite perceptive. He said that a disadvantage of home education is the lack of acceptance of home schooling by society. When this book was first written, 1985, this was probably true. Home schooling was doing something different than neighbors and friends. But now it has become so much more common that everyone we meet knows at least one home schooler, and rarely do we see any disapproval. Usually there's a lot of curiosity, but the general public is beginning to have a positive general attitude about the great advantages of a home education.

QUESTION #6: THE ADVANTAGES OF HOME SCHOOLING ARE:
(check as many as apply)

Total   Response

41%   The parents are able to monitor the child's progress better than a teacher because the parents has more time for individual attention.
        [Urban 25%, rural 53%]
        [Administrators 33%, teachers 50%]

41%   This type of education provides a unique parent-child bonding.
        [Urban 25%, rural 53%]

31%   The parents re-educate themselves as they educate their children.
        [Urban 17%, rural 41%]
        [Administrators 20%, teachers 43%]

7%   The children receive a better education at home.
        [All rural teachers]

62%   The children are able to have time to develop their interests, talents, and hobbies.
        [Urban 50%, rural 71%]
        [Administrators 47%, teachers 79%]

Numbers add to more than 100% because more than one response could be checked.

The purpose of this question was to see which, if any, positive qualities educators would attribute to home schools. The major advantage, they believe, is time for children to develop their creative interests. It's really an admission that schools stifle creativity and individuality, which they do (Chapter 2). Teachers are more aware of it than administrators, probably because of their connection with actual classroom experience. Teachers are also more aware of the importance of individual attention that the immediacy of feedback in the home school permits.

Few educators believe that children could receive a better education at home, but home school academic successes abound.

SUMMARY

Teachers are people too. They really are. The criticisms of public education in this book are not intended as a slight on any individual educator or on educators as a group. I have no personal axe to grind. The problems are due to the system, to the institution that has been created over the past 200 years.

The mountains of problems with public schools are the result of the way that the system has developed, especially since the Industrial Revolution. The problems are serious because they are so deeply entrenched in the philosophical and ideological foundations of American public education. If any particular teacher seems to be a prime example of these shortcomings, just remember: that person is a product of the system too!

Today's teachers are simply last generation's students who have reversed roles. They cannot be any different than the way they are because it's the only way they know.

Many home schoolers are teachers, administrators, and former teachers, which seems to indicate that some teachers really do care about children. Some teachers really do want children to learn. There are even a few of them who realize that students are individuals. But it's nearly impossible to carry out those beliefs into practice within the current system.

When educators react negatively to home schools, what are they afraid of? Possible explanations are:

HOME SCHOOLS: An Alternative

1. **Fear of a drop in enrollment.** Administrators and teachers both fear any further drop in enrollment after the recent decline because of the tapering off of the Baby Boom. Fewer students means less funding, which means that fewer teachers would be needed.

Fewer students = Less funding = Fewer teachers

They think that encouraging home schools would lead to a drastic drop in school enrollment. Nobody wants to lose his job because he is no longer needed. These fears, however, are unfounded because even the most friendly atmosphere would not change the reasons why parents choose home education, and only a small percentage of people would ever have the commitment it takes to educate their own children.

2. **Fear of the audit trail.** The endless paperwork for administrators and teachers is a headache. It's also unfair to them. They are expected to keep track of every student in every way. If they don't, they can lose funding. Administrators fear more paperwork due to home schoolers, with equal accountability.

3. **Fear of the loss of prestige.** Educators may feel that they will lose prestige if they admit that anyone can teach, not just certified teachers.

4. **Fear of admitting that public schools have problems.** Administrators may feel that cooperating with home schoolers is equal to admitting that public schools are inadequate.

Solutions to these problems are really quite simple. Home schoolers should be required to report only to the State Department of Education, and still be counted in the district's head count. That way administrators need not fear accountability for home schoolers, nor declining enrollment. Funding and paperwork would not change in the local district due to home schools. This solution would also encourage cooperation between schools and home educators since the schools would already be receiving the funding to do so.

These are some of the bureaucratic answers available. Other solutions will come only with a change in the attitudes of educators towards education, its purpose, and the people for whom it was intended. After all, our children are people too!

CHAPTER TWELVE
Help for the Home Schooler

Many parents have asked me how to find good resources. This chapter shows how to get started, even if you're going to develop your own curriculum. The first couple of months of planning curriculum are the hardest, but you soon get used to it. Once you know your child's educational level, it becomes as easy as putting on shoes. Another very useful book for someone interested in home schooling is *Home Education Resource Guide,* available from Blue Bird Publishing, and there's an order form at the end of this book.

The first step is to get an idea of what a typical school curriculum is for your child's grade level. You can write to Educational Services Department, World Book Educational Products, 101 Northwest Point Blvd., Elk Grove Village IL 60007 for their brochure, "Typical Course for Study, K-12." This curriculum outline has been reprinted in the book *The Home School Manual* (5th Edition) by Ted Wade. Or check with your local home schooling organization and chat with parents who have children the same age as yours.

The idea is to get a grasp on what children of that age group typically are taught in local schools. For instance, you should know whether multiplication is taught in second, third, or fourth grade.

Good starter material is published by ESP (address later in chapter). Each of these workbooks is inexpensive and sequentially teaches the same basic materials that the child would be taught in public schools. As you become more comfortable with the subject matter at a grade level, you will want to supplement it with other materials and activities.

A home education can be as expensive or as inexpensive as you want to make it. Some people spend nearly nothing on materials, using the library constantly. Others spend much more, especially if they are using correspondence schools. Still others start by using a correspondence school until they feel comfortable with teaching, then select their own materials.

You can save money by swapping materials with other home schoolers. It's another good reason to join a local organization. Some organizations have a reference library. They can also offer teaching suggestions. Home schooling newsletters and magazines provide additional valuable information about where to obtain materials and suggestions on teaching.

A private school teacher told me how she gathered textbooks for a newly-established private school. She asked several public and private schools if they had materials in their "Resource Room" that they would sell. Every school has a roomful of used books, sometimes dated textbooks, sometimes new textbooks that they decided not to use after buying them, and other materials. Some schools are willing to sell these; some will lend them to you while others will not.

Many people have found that once they have an overview of a year's coursework, they can break it down into weekly guidelines. These guidelines can be as formal or as informal as the parent chooses. An example of a formal guideline with informal approaches to certain subjects looks like this:

WEEK OF DECEMBER 15-DECEMBER 21

1. MATH
> Fractions book, pages 10-13
> Multiplication book, pages 55-58
> Look at measurements: Pour quarts into pints,
> then change into liters; measure the house in
> feet, then change to yards. Discuss how we
> use measurements in cooking and drawing.

2. SPELLING & PHONICS
> Review blends "br" and "sl"

Spell Christmas words we listed

3. WRITING & HANDWRITING

Write letter to Grandpa and Grandma in cursive, using some of the spelling words for this week.
Discuss Christmas topics, then choose one to write about.

4. READING

Read "A Christmas Carol" by Dickens
Discuss the differences in culture from the Dickensian period to now; is Christmas celebrated differently?
Discuss the moral implications in the story.

5. SCIENCE

Take a nature walk and identify footprints in the snow.
Look in the encyclopedia to find how snow is made.
Discuss good health habits in cold weather.

6. SOCIAL SCIENCE

Look at the globe and discuss why we have snow while Southern Hemisphere has summer.
Discuss Christmas and holiday customs in different countries.
Talk about what winter was like for the Pilgrims and the American Indians.

7. ART

Make homemade Christmas decorations together.

8. MUSIC

We're going to a holiday concert.

9. OTHER

> Household chores: learning to bake our tradi-
> tional holiday cookies, then cleaning up
> afterward.

I found it handy to write an overview of what I expected my daughter to accomplish in a year's time. With that overview in mind, I could then break down monthly and weekly objectives. This may sound very structured or complicated at first, but it's really as simple as:

> *This year we will put added emphasis on spelling. By*
> *May, I expect that she will be able to spell better*
> *overall by studying common forms and also excep-*
> *tions to the rules. During the first month, we will study*
> *the -tion words. Second month, how to form plurals.*
> *Third month, how to form possessives. Plus a word list*
> *each week of 30 words to study and use in sentences.*
> *This will increase vocabulary as well as spelling.*

If you desire more complicated record-keeping, or if it's required by your state, a good resource for forms is *Home School: Taking the First Step* by Borg Hendrickson.

The rest of this chapter is divided according to these types of resources to use in home schooling:

1. Magazines for children
2. Textbooks and educational materials
3. Games
4. Computer games and instruction
5. Other learning experiences
6. Correspondence schools
7. Newsletters and magazines for home schooling
8. Other important addresses.

Longer lists of these are available in the book, *Home Education Resource*

Guide, also from Blue Bird Publishing. (Order form at the end of the book.) That book also contains other valuable information such as reading lists, Bible education and Christian materials, child training books, how-to-home-school books, help for the handicapped, music education, and audio-visual materials.

MAGAZINES

The beauty of using magazines for an educational resource is that the material can be geared to each child's interests such as wildlife, general science, history or writing. The magazines present the subjects in a fresh way, unlike the way they are presented in most textbooks.

Another plus for children's magazines is that many of them encourage reader participation. My daughter had a poem published in one of the magazines by the Children's Better Health Institute.

Check your local library for the magazines they carry. Ask them to order any that your children might enjoy. Libraries encourage ideas from their patrons, and will probably be happy to help. To find more children's magazines, look at the listings in the *Children's Magazine Guide,* found in the reference section.

A few excellent magazines are listed here:

Boy's Life
Published by the Boy Scouts of America, Magazine Division, 1325 Walnut Hill Lane, Irving TX 75038-3096. (214) 580-2000. Subscription: $7.80 to Boy Scouts, $15.60 per year (12 issues) to others.

Children's Better Health Institute, 1100 Waterway Blvd., Indianapolis IN 46206. (317) 636-8881. This company publishes several good children's magazines. Health, fitness, and good habits are stressed but are not the only topics. Children may participate by sending pictures and stories.

Child Life, ages 10-14.
Children's Digest, ages 8-12.
Children's Playmate, ages 5-9.
Humpty Dumpty, ages 5-9.
Jack and Jill, ages 7-11.
Turtle, preschool.

U*S*KIDS, A Weekly Reader Magazine, ages 5-10.

Children's Television Workshop, 1 Lincoln Plaza, New York NY 10023. Orders toll-free 1-800-678-0613. Phone (212) 595-3456.
> *Sesame Street,* ages 2-6, $19.90, 1 year, 10 issues.
> *Kid City,* ages 6-10, $16.97, 1 year, 10 issues.
> *3-2-1 Contact,* ages 8-14, $17.97, 1 year, 10 issues.

Cobblestone Publications, Inc., 7 School St., Peterborough NH 03458, (603) 924-7209. Web Site: http:/www.cobblestonepub.com
> *Calliope,* world history grades, 4-9, $18.95, 1 year, 5 issues.
> *Faces,* world cultures, grades 4-9, $23.95, 1 year, 9 issues.
> *Cobblestone,* American history, grades 4-9, $24.95, 1 year, 9 issues.
> *Odyssey,* science, grades 4-9, $24.95, 1 year, 9 issues.

Concord Review: A Quarterly Review of Essays by Students of History
Write: PO Box 661, Concord MA 01742. (508) 331-5007. Email: fitzhugh@tcr.org
The Concord Review is the only journal in the world to publish the academic work of secondary students. Since 1987, they have published 286 history essays from student authors in the United States and 19 other countries. Many of the students have sent reprints of their essays with their college applications. They welcome materials from homeschooled students. **See ad page 157.**

Cricket Magazine Group, PO Box 7434, Red Oak IA 51591-4434. 1-800-827-0227. Cost $2.75 per issue, each magazine.
> *Babybug,* 6 months to two years, 9 issues a year.
> *Ladybug,* ages 2-6, 12 issues a year.
> *Spider,* ages 6-9, 12 issues a year.
> *Cricket,* ages 9-14, 12 issues a year.

Highlights for Children
Write: 2300 West Fifth Ave., PO Box 269, Columbus OH 43272-0002. Toll-free 1-800-255-9517. Cost: $29.64 for 1 year, 12 issues, ages 5-12. This magazine has been thrilling children for two generations with stories, cartoons, activities, and submissions from readers. It's a five-star children's magazine.

National Geographic, 1145 17th St. NW, Washington DC 20036 (202) 857-7000.
> *National Geographic.* This magazine has been a delight for generations. The photography is top-notch and the scientific articles are well-researched and well-written. Although the vocabulary is too advanced

for young readers, the pictures help them explore lands and cultures far away or in their own backyard.

National Geographic World. Topics in science and social science, with special inputs such as "KIDS DID IT!" page with features on thigns such as young auctioneers and cartoonists. Children can participate in cartoons and art. Naturally the magazine is up to the high standards of the National Geographic Society.

National Wildlife Federation, 1400 16th Street NW, Washington DC 20036. Order toll-free 1-800-432-6564. Customer service toll-free 1-800-822-9919. TDD toll-free 1-800-435-3543.

Ranger Rick, ages 6-12, $15, 12 issues.

Your Big Backyard, ages 3-5, $14, 12 issues.

Scienceland

Write: 501 Fifth Ave., New York NY 10017. (212) 490-2180. Cost: $36 (1 yr), ages 6-11.

Stone Soup

Write: Children's Art Foundation, PO Box 83, Santa Cruz CA 95063. (408) 426-5557. Cost: $26/ 5 issues (1 yr), ages 6-12. This magazine was one of my daughter's favorites as a child. It is totally devoted to publishing writing by children for children. It is designed to be an inspiration for their creative energies, and it really works! Kids can see what other kids are writing, and then compare their own writing to what they see. They can also submit stories to the magazine for possible publication. The magazine's emphasis is on non-fiction.

Weekly Reader

Weekly Reader Corporation, 245 Long Hill Road, PO Box 2791, Middletown CT 06457-9291. Toll-free customer service 1-800-446-3355. The ever-popular *Weekly Reader* is available for Pre-K through grade 6. The minimum order is for 10 students, so homeschoolers should order with their homeschool support group, if interested.

Zillions

Editorial Address: Consumers Union of US Inc., PO Box 57777, Yonkers NY 10703. (914) 378-2000. This magazine was formerly called *Penny Power*. Cost: $16 for one year, 6 issues. Ages 7-12. This is a great magazine for consumer education for children. Too many times children are not taught how to handle themselves in the marketplace, or how to conduct a simple business transaction like an adult. This magazine helps, with articles such as "They Won't Wait on Me ... and Other Problems Kids Have in Stores" and "Do Toys Live Up to Their TV Commercials?"

TEXTBOOKS AND SCHOOL MATERIALS

Write for a catalog from the companies that suit your needs. Be sure to specify if you are interested in elementary or secondary school materials, or both. I've found that most textbook companies are willing to sell to individuals, but it may cost you a little more than it would cost a school.

The aspect that I find most disappointing about educational materials is that few of them are developed for older children, except for conventional textbooks. Everyone likes to develop fun ways to learn for younger children, but it's very difficult to find exciting educational materials for children at the junior high level or older. I hope that the manufacturers of these materials will soon address this issue, and make learning fun for older children and adults.

A Beka Book
PO Box 18000, Pensacola FL 32523-9160. (904) 478-8933. Christian and traditional approach in all subjects for preschool through 12th grade.

Allied Educational Press
PO Box 737, Niles MI 49120, (616) 684-7855. Remedial and beginning reading, grammar and math. Most books very reasonably priced..

Backyard Scientist
PO Box 16966, Irvine CA 92713. Science books for ages 4-12 with hands-on experiments; a home school classic.

Bluestocking Press
PO Box 2030, Shingle Springs CA 95682-2030. (916) 621-1123. Toll-free 1-800-959-8586. FAX (916) 642-9222. *Bluestocking Press Resource Guide and Catalog* ($3) lists over 1,000 items with a concentration on American history, economics, and law. This is an excellent source for supplementary materials in those areas. **See ad page 159.**

Christian Curriculum Project
2006 Flat Creek, Richardson TX 75080. Christian-oriented math, music, and textbooks.

Christian Light Publications
PO Box 1212, Harrisonburg VA 22801. (540) 434-0750. Christian curriculum for grades 1-12, high school diplomas.

Cuisenaire Company
10 Bank St., White Plains NY 10602. (914) 997-2600. Source for Cuisenaire rods for learning math. Has added other products for learning math and science.

ESP
7163 123rd Circle N., Largo FL 34643. 1-800-643-0280. Has a set of elementary and kindergarten "super-workbooks," each of which will teach sequentially the basic subject matter taught by public schools. Good inexpensive starter material.

Gazelle Publications
9853 Jericho Road, Bridgman MI 49106-9742. (616) 465-4004. Toll-free 1-800-650-5076. E-mail: wadeted@aol.com   This company publishes *The Home School Manual* by Ted Wade and 17 others. This book is now in its 6th edition ($24.95) and is a must for homeschoolers. It's also available now on 2 diskettes for Windows, $16. **See ad page 160.**

Golden Books Publishing
1220 Mound Avenue, Racine WI 53404, (414) 633-2431. The "Golden Step Ahead®" series of workbooks is excellent and inexpensive. They are designed in a format that is ideal for home schoolers. They can often be found locally in supermarkets and department stores. Reading, writing, spelling, math, science, and social science. The catalog lists other preschool and elementary materials as well.

Gryphon House
10726 Tucker St., PO Box 207, Beltsville MD 20704. (301) 779-6200. Early childhood reading books. Books about feelings, growing, and family.

Holcomb & Company
PO Box 94636, Cleveland OH 44101. Toll-free 1-800-362-9907. I can't even begin to describe the materials available from Holcomb, but there is everything you ever wanted for creative, fun learning from preschool through elementary school. Arts and crafts , templates, filmstrip maker kit, records, books, musical instruments, thinking games, science projects (ant farm, greenhouse, aquarium, dinosaur models), math games (abacus, beads, clocks, calendars, measurements, Cuisenaire rods, fractions, play money, calculators, play checkbooks), language and phonics, computer software, and social studies (puzzle maps, globes).

Holt Associates
John Holt's Bookstore, 2269 Massachusetts Ave., Cambridge MA 02140. (617) 864-3100. Books and products for home schooling parents and children. **See ad page 159.**

Houghton Mifflin
2 Park Street, Boston MA 02108, (617) 725-5000. Major textbook publisher, both elementary and secondary.

Jordan's Knowledge Nook
2400 Judson Road, Longview TX 75605. (903) 753-8741. Toll-free 1-800-562-5490. FAX (903) 757-6980. The Knowledge Nook puts out a comprehensive mail-order line which includes Milton Bradley/ Playskool, Carson Dellosa Publishing, Dennison Manufacturing Company, Educational Service, Learning Works, Melody House Records, Millikin Publishing/ Timesaver for Teachers, Peck, Frank Schaffer Publications, and Trend Enterprises. The catalog is an inch thick and has everything from art supplies to computer programs. There are sticker collections, which are good little rewards for work well done. Materials for math, science, social science, and language arts.

Konos Curriculum
PO Box 1534, Richardson TX 75083 (214) 669-8337. A character-building curriculum designed for home schools.

Leonardo Press
PO Box 1326, Camden ME 04843. Spelling and phonics programs.

Library and Educational Services
8784 Valley View Drive, PO Box 146, Berrien Springs MI 49103, (616) 471-1400. Catalog of home schooling, educational, and reading books.

Living Heritage Academy
PO Box 299000, Lewisville TX 75029-9000, (214) 462-1776. Christian curriculum K-12.

McGraw-Hill Book Company
Webster Division, 1221 Avenue of the Americas, New York NY 10020. (212) 512-2000. Major conventional textbook publisher for elementary and high school.

NASCO
PO Box 3837, Modesto CA 95352-3837. 1-800-558-9595. A mail-order source for

books and materials. Includes language arts, social studies, reading books, arts and crafts, music, science, math, computer, and health.

National Textbook Company
4255 West Touhy Ave., Lincolnwood Chicago IL 60646 (847) 679-5500. Reading and writing skills development for high school. Also theater arts, debate, speech, journalism, and mass media.

Rod & Staff Publishers
Highway 172, Crockett KY 41413. (606) 522-4348. Christian curriculum materials.

Sadlier-Oxford
9 Pine St., New York NY 10005, (212) 227-2120. Textbooks for elementary and secondary. Spelling, math, vocabulary, and social studies. Inexpensive. Has a special catalog for Christian educational materials. I've personally used their "New Progress in Mathematics" series and have been very pleased with it.

School Zone Publishing Company
1819 Industrial Drive, PO Box 777, Grand Haven MI 49417, (616) 846-5030. Internet site: http://www.schoolzone.com   The "School Zone®" series is great for home schoolers. There is a preschool series and an elementary series. There are short, inexpensive workbooks in math, handwriting, phonics, reading, spelling, grammar, motor skills, perceptual skills, and general learning. These books are often found in supermarkets and larger chain drugstores, or you can order directly from the company.

Scott, Foresman & Company
1900 East Lake Ave., Glenview IL 60025. Toll-free 1-800-554-4411. Major traditional textbook publisher for elementary and junior high level texts.

SRA
70 West Madison, Suite 1400, Chicago IL 60602.(312) 214-7250. SRA is number one in the field of individualized learning. Their reading labs are exceptionally well designed for children. They have also developed individualized instruction for math and social science. I highly recommend the reading lab, but a major drawback is its price. A suggestion is to share the cost with other home schoolers.

SUA Phonics
1339 E MacMillan St, Cincinnati OH 45206. Phonics program—inexpensive and highly recommended.

Summit Christian Academy
ZFW Corporate Park, 2100 N. Hwy 360 #503, Grand Prairie TX 75050. Orders: 1-800-362-9180. Bible-based home school curriculum K-12.

Sycamore Tree Inc.
2179 Meyer Place, Costa Mesa CA 92627, (714) 650-4466. A large catalog full of Christian and home schooling materials: Bible materials, character development, reading, math, grammar, spelling, social studies, science, foreign language, sex education, physical education, arts & crafts, music, cooking, computer education, games and more! **See ad page 160.**

The Timberdoodle
East 1610 Spencer Lake Road, Shelton WA 98584, (360) 426-0672. FAX (360) 427-5627. Toll-free ordering 1-800-478-0672. Email: mailbag@timberdoodle.com Internet site: http://www.timberdoodle.com Puzzles, Cuisenaire rods, educational coloring books, workbooks.

Thompson's Depository
39 NE 24th, PO Box 60160, Oklahoma City OK 73146 (PO Box) Zip for street address is 73105. (405) 525-9458. For individuals within the state of Oklahoma, they can provide materials for K-12.

GAMES

Games are a fun way to learn, and there are many possibilities. Suggestions include:

> hangman (for spelling)
> chess (logic and strategy)
> checkers (logic)
> crossword puzzles (vocabulary and spelling)
> Clue®
> Upwords®
> Stratego®
> Battleship®
> Connect Four®
> Simon®

Many companies are now developing simulation games, which are good if you have several children. A simulation game gives students the chance to pretend that they are in a situation and they need to figure out certain strategies. Games that teach government and economics are popular.

More sources for games are listed below. A more extensive listing of games and toys is found in *Home Education Resource Guide*, which can be ordered on the last page of this book through Blue Bird Publishing.

Allied Educational Press
PO Box 737, Niles MI 49120, (616) 684-7855. Individualized reading games.

Ampersand Press
750 Lake St., Port Townsend WA 98368, Orders toll-free 1-800-624-4263. Phone (360) 379-5187 FAX (360) 379-0324. Science & nature learning games. Also games on geometry and electrical circuitry.

Animal Town Game Company
PO Box 485, Healdsburg CA 95448. Toll-free 1-800-445-8642. Carrying cooperative and noncompetitive games, board games about nature and living.

Aristoplay
PO Box 7028, Ann Arbor MI 48107, 1-800-634-7738. Games for learning art, music, history, prehistory, world peace, and more.

Interact
1825 Gillespie Way #101, El Cajon CA 92020-1095. (619) 448-1474. Most of the simulation games are for groups, but there are many good ones: "Newscast," a simulation of a TV news team's coverage of a historic event, $53; "Empathy," what it's like to be physically handicapped; and many more involving literature, history, geography, health, law, and economics, $51.

WFF 'N PROOF
1490 South Boulevard, Ann Arbor MI 48104-4699, (313) 665-2269. Inexpensive educational games that teach logic, science, word structures, geometry, mathematics, set theory, social studies, problem solving, arithmetic and strategy. Equations games for the computer—IBM or Macintosh. Satisfaction guaranteed. Ask for catalog.

COMPUTER PROGRAMS

Our children will be lost in the future if they do not become computer literate. They must become comfortable with the operation and language of computers. There are, surprisingly, moderately priced computers on the market today, with prices becoming more reasonable each year. More and more educationally oriented programs are developed each year. Be sure to check the availability of the types of programs you want before you select your computer, or you may end up with a computer that doesn't do what you want it to do. I've known parents who have purchased a computer that played a lot of games, but basically had no other purpose. That's too limiting.

The Internet is the big craze now. Your children can learn to access unlimited amounts of information on the Internet, and use it for research. E-mail seems to be the communication network of the future, and it's good for children to learn how to do it. Of course, I suggest monitoring what they are actually viewing online.

Children are adept at computer programming. It's easiest when introduced little by little when they're young. Although not every one of them will choose to become computer wizards, they will know how to work with the computer, and how to communicate in a computer world. The important thing is for them to become comfortable with computers, and not to be frightened of the machine. I've seen many older adults who are so intimidated by the idea of computers that they cannot even read a simple computer printout, yet they can handle the most complicated accounting transaction. This will not happen with youngsters who are able to interact with computers starting at a young age.

Video games for the computer are sometimes more educational than you realize. One game that I had for an earlier model computer was "Taxman." It is fun yet it teaches prime numbers. There's a typing game on my current computer, and it was the incentive behind my daughter's desire to learn to type. Children who play games on the computer learn to be at ease with the machine, and adjust quickly to other types of computer activities.

These companies have educational computer programs. Detailed information is available in the *Home Education Resource Guide*, which can be ordered on the last page of this book through Blue Bird Publishing.

Davidson & Associates, PO Box 2961, Torrance CA 90509. Call toll-free 1-800-545-7677 to ask for the authorized dealer near you. Many stores carry their very popular products.

HEC Reading Horizons, 3471 South 550 West, Bountiful UT 84010. Toll-free 1-800-333-0059. Phonics computer courses.

MacSoft, ask for catalog, 1-800-229-2714.

Meridian Creative Group, 5178 Station Road, Erie PA 16510-4636. Order toll-free 1-800-695-9427. Phone (814) 898-26112. FAX (814) 898-0683.

Mindscape, 88 Rowland Way, Novato CA 94945. Orders toll-free 1-800-231-3088.

Motes Educational Software, PO Box 575, Siloam Springs AR 72761. (501) 524-8741.

Nordic Software, PO Box 6007, Lincoln NE 68506-0007. Phone (402) 488-5086. FAX (402) 488-2914. Web Site://www.nordicsoftware.com/

novaNet Campus, University Communications, Inc., 3895 N. Business Center Drive, Suite 120, Tucson AZ 85705. Orders toll-free 1-800-243-7758. Phone (520) 888-3076. FAX (520) 888-8729.

Packard Bell Interactive, 1201 Third Ave., Suite 2301, Seattle WA 98101. (206) 654-4100. Their educational software is available nationally through retail channels, or call for catalog.

Sound Software, 3905 Coronado, Plano TX 75074. (214) 516-1328.

OTHER LEARNING EXPERIENCES

Once you start developing ideas on how many different ways there are to learn, then education can become very exciting. Parents who educate their own children can learn for themselves that education need not be painful, that learning can indeed be fun.

Field trips are great, but unfortunately in school they are rush-rush and don't-touch. Field trips with the family are relaxed and can really add to the child's knowledge of the world around him.

Many cities, such as Indianapolis and Boston, now have Children's Museums. In these museums, many of the displays are designed to be touched, to be played with, and to be experienced. For example, the Indianapolis Children's Museum has a simulated cave that visitors can walk through. The feel, smell, and sounds are exactly like a local Indiana cave.

Outings such as spelunking, a hike, or a nature walk are a part of physical education as well as learning. Another suggestion is to show your children how and where people work. That's more effective than any guidance counselor in the world. People are an important resource when it comes to understanding the world.

Theaters and lectures are valuable for keeping up with our culture and business. Orlando is one area that has many theater performances and lectures designed especially for children. Many areas have special attrractions, such as Fort Lauderdale's Discovery Place, for children. Special lectures and displays are designed to teach certain subjects. For instance, there has been a special computer exposition at the Discovery Place, and the children were able to use computers for graphic design. They also could talk to experienced computer graphic artists.

Special events are valuable learning experiences: trips to gift shows, auto shows, recreational shows, boat shows, antique shows, graphic arts shows, book shows. All of these can teach about our business and culture better than any book. State and local fairs have wonderful exhibits, such as agricultural, photography, and crafts. Art shows reflect the creative impulses in our society.

Television is coming of age in regard to quality educational programming. In urban areas you have your choice of superb programs nearly every hour of the day. In rural areas, cable television is now narrowing the gap of what is available there compared to cities. PBS offers *Nova* and *Wonderworks.* The Discovery Channel offers numerous programs about different cultures around the world and travel programs. For New Year's Eve, there were 30-minute features about special celebrations in places such as Morocco, Spain, the Canary Islands, and Tahiti. Keep track of what the stations are showing; you'd be remarkably surprised that your children might show a preference for this type of programming.

Group activities will help the children learn as well as provide social interaction. Such groups as 4-H, Girl Scouts, Boy Scouts, Campfire Girls, church groups, musical groups, community groups, and physical education are the kinds of social activities that parents find suitable. Be sure to include activities that develop your child's special talents. Older children can join specialized organizations, such as environmental groups, spelunking groups, archaeological groups, theater groups, etc.

Work is the ultimate learning experience, and we shouldn't deny it to our children. They should all have their daily and weekly household chores. Baking, gardening, taking care of pets, and cleaning are all great ideas for learning the joy of work.

And by all means, don't forget the LIBRARY! You'll be amazed at the types of activities now available through your local library, including author's appearances, story sessions for children, lending of video tapes, lending of audio tapes, and special events.

CORRESPONDENCE SCHOOLS

For a directory of home study schools, write the National Home Study Council, 1601 18th St NW, Washington DC 20009.

Alpha Omega Publications
PO Box 3153, Tempe AZ 85281, (602) 438-1092. Christian correspondence programs, plus a full catalog of curriculum materials. Call 1-800-821-4443.

American School
850 East 58th St, Chicago IL 60637, (312) 947-3300. High school correspondence program.

Bob Jones University Press
Greenville SC 29614. 1-800-845-5731 (toll free outside SC). 1-803-242-5100, ext 4300 (for use in SC and Canada). Complete curriculum grades K4-12, Christian orientation.

Brigham Young University
Department of Independent Study, 206 Harman Continuing Education Building, Provo UT 84602, (801) 378-2868.

Calvert School
105 Tuscany Road, Baltimore MD 21210, (301) 243-6030.

Christian Liberty Academy
502 West Euclid Avenue, Arlington Heights IL 60004, (312) 259-8736.

Clonlara Home-Based Education Program
1289 Jewett, Ann Arbor MI 48104, (313) 769-4515.

Hewitt Homeschooling Resources
PO Box 9, Washougal WA 98671-0009. (360) 835-8708. FAX (360) 835-8697.
PO Box 92, Escondido CA 92025, (619) 749-92025. High school program.

Home Study International
12501 Old Columbia Pike, Silver Spring MD 20904-6600. (301) 680-6570. FAX (301) 680-6577. Toll-free 1-800-782-GROW (4769).

Phoenix Special Programs
Correspondence Study, 3132 West Clarendon Avenue, Phoenix AZ 85017-4589. (602) 263-5661. High school correspondence program, available to all states.

Seton Home Study School
1350 Progress Driv, , Front Royal VA 22630, (540) 636-9990. Catholic high school program.

University of Nebraska—Lincoln
Independent Study High School, 33rd and Holdredge Streets, Lincoln NE 68583-0900. (402) 472-1926. High school home study.

University of Missouri Center for Independent Study
136 Clark Hall, Columbia MD 65211. Toll-free 1-800-609-3727. High school home study. **See ad page 158.**

HOME SCHOOL MAGAZINES & NEWSLETTERS

Arizona Families for Home Education, PO Box 4661, Scottsdale AZ 85261-4661. (602) 860-2437. Newsletter, 4 pages, $8 a year/ 5 issues.

Bob Jones University Press, Greenville SC 29614. 1-800-845-5731 (toll-free number for outside SC). 1-803-242-5100, extension 4300 (for use in South Carolina & Canada). "Home School Helper" newsletter is provided free four times a year to give homeschoolers useful tips for teaching and news of interest. Call toll-free number for subscription.

Catholic Home School Newsletter, 688 11th Ave NW, New Brighton MN 55112. (612) 636-5761. The Catholic Home School Newsletter is a one-page newsletter with information specifically for Catholic homeschoolers. Mailed three times a year. Back issues for 45¢ postage and self-addressed envelope.

Christian Life Workshops, PO Box 2250, Gresham OR 97030. (503) 667-3942. Publishes the *Our Family Favorites* catalog yearly, no charge.

Holt Associates, 2269 Massachusetts Ave., Cambridge MA 02140. (617) 864-3100. Publishers of the national homeschooling newsletter *Growing Without Schooling* since 1977. Very useful and highly recommended. $20 for 6 issues/ 1 year. Back issues still available. Single issue $3.

Home Education Press, PO Box 1083, 1814 Hiway 20 E., Tonasket WA 98855. Internet site: http://www.home-edpress.com   This company publishes *Home Education Magazine*, an excellent well-rounded national homeschooling magazine. There is something for everyone in this publication. $24 for 6 issues. Current issue, first class, $4.50. Other home schooling products available from this company. **See ad page 158.**

Home Educators Association of Virginia, PO Box 6745, Richmond VA 23230-0745. (804) 288-1608. FAX (804) 288-6962. Email: heav33@aol.cpm Publishes *The Virginia Home Educator*, a monthly newsletter for members—membership $25 per year per family.

Home Schools United—Vegas Valley, PO Box 93564, Las Vegas NV 89193. (702) 870-9566. Newsletter is $15 for 12 monthly issues.

National Home Education Research Institute, ATTN: Dr. Brian Ray, Western

Baptist College, 5000 Deer Park Dr. SE, Salem OR 97301-9392. (503) 375-7019. Publishes *Home School Researcher*, an academic quarterly. $25 per year subscription rate.

Pennsylvania Homeschoolers, RD 2 Box 117, Kittanning PA 16201. (412) 783-6512. Publishes a newsletter four times a year as a statewide network for sharing information about home education. Approximately 28 pages per issue. Subscription: $8..

Teaching Home, PO Box 20219, Portland OR 97220-0219. (503) 253-9633. Subscription address: PO Box 469069, Escondido CA 92046-9069. 1-800-395-7760. A national Christian homeschooling magazine, published bimonthly. Many state newsletters are co-published within this magazine, making it a very convenient package. Trial subscription available with no payment due until after first issue has been examined. All back issues still available.

Unschoolers Network, 2 Smith Street, Farmingdale NJ 07727. (201) 938-2473. Newsletter 3 times a year, bulletin in other months—$12 a year. SASE for list of materials and products available.

Wisdom's Gate, Home School Digest, PO Box 125, Sawyer MI 49125. *Home School Digest* is a quarterly national magazine with numerous informative articles about the different aspects of home schooling. Includes a special calendar of events. Subscription: $10 per year. **See ad page 161.**

OTHER IMPORTANT ADDRESSES

EVAN-G, the Committee to End Violence Against the Next Generation, Inc., 977 Keeler Ave., Berkeley CA 94708. (510) 527-0454 This group is dedicated to eliminating corporal punishment in the public schools and to ending all forms of violence against children.

The Mel Gablers, PO Box 7518. Longview TX 75607. (903) 753-5993. The Gablers have a national textbook review clearing house. Reviews furnished for donations.

THE CONCORD REVIEW—VARSITY ACADEMICS

The Concord Review, Inc., was founded, in March 1987, to search out and publish exemplary history essays by high-school students in the English-speaking world. With the twenty-sixth issue (special AP issue for the College Board), 286 papers (average 5,000 words) have been published from authors in thirty-two states and nineteen other countries (Argentina, Australia, Brazil, Canada, Chile, England, Finland, France, Germany, Greece, Holland, Indonesia, Ireland, Japan, Kenya, Morocco, Norway, Singapore and Wales). As of May 1996, *The Concord Review* remains the only journal in the world to publish the academic work of secondary students.

The work of these students has earned recognition from James Fallows, Chester E. Finn, Jr., Harold Howe II, David McCullough, Diane Ravitch, Albert Shanker, Theodore Sizer, Donald Stewart, the American Textbook Council, the Educational Excellence Network, the National Council for History Education, the New England History Teachers Association, and many others.

Many of our authors have sent reprints of their articles with their college application materials, and they have gone on to Berkeley(5), Brown(9), Columbia(6), Cornell(7), Dartmouth(3), Harvard(34), Oxford(6), Pennsylvania(5), Princeton(9), Stanford(5), Yale(28), and a number of other fine institutions, including Cal Tech, Cambridge, McGill, and MIT.

We have sent such exemplary history essays to subscribers (students, teachers and librarians) in forty-two states and thirty countries (Argentina, Australia, Austria, Belgium, Brazil, Canada, Chile, Colombia, England, France, Greece, Holland, India, Indonesia, Ireland, Israel, Italy, Japan, Kenya, Malaysia, Mexico, New Guinea, New Zealand, Paraguay, Saudi Arabia, Singapore, South Africa, Switzerland, Turkey and Wales. Teachers in many schools are using these essays as examples of good historical writing.

We welcome serious history essays from *homescholars* and we need subscriptions from their teachers. 🍂

The Concord Review • Post Office Box 661, Concord, MA 01742
(800) 331-5007 INTERNET: fitzhugh@tcr.org WEBSITE: http://www.tcr.org

Dr. Christman's LEARN TO READ BOOK
by Dr. Ernest Christman

A complete learn-to-read program for all ages.
This highly illustrated book is a fun, yet effective
way to teach anyone to read. Step-by-step the
book uses the best building blocks for learning
how to read.

ISBN 0-933025-17-3   256 pages $15.95

APPENDIX
HOME SCHOOL SUPPORT GROUPS
& NATIONAL ORGANIZATIONS

National

Christian Life Workshops (CLW), Box 2250, Gresham OR 97030. (503) 667-3942. This organization is a national organization with chapters across the United States and some in Great Britain. Their magazine/catalog offers a wide variety of materials to order and articles to read.

HCL, PO Box 4643, Whittier CA 90607. (310) 696-4696. This is not a support group, but rather an administrative unit serving families in California and nationwide. This organization provides standard private school services such as transferring of records, maintenance of cumulative files, course of study requirements and educational resource recommendations. It also offers a high school diploma program.

Holt Associates, 2269 Massachusetts Ave, Cambridge MA 02140. (617) 864-3100. FAX (617) 864-9235. John Holt is considered the father of modern homeschooling. If you're reading this book, you've no doubt heard much about him. He authored ten books about education including the classic, *How Children Fail*. In 1977 he founded *Growing Without Schooling*, a newsletter dedicated to supporting home educators. He also founded John Holt's Bookstore, a catalog through which he sold books about education that he thought were especially good.

This organization is not a local homeschool support group, but rather an organization that supports homeschooling nationally.

Homeschool Associates, 116 Third Avenue, Auburn ME 04210. (207) 777-1700, (207) 777-0077. FAX: (207) 777-1776. This group is very active. They hold conferences such as the Detroit/ Midwest Homeschool Conference in August and others. At the 1993 conference, the featured speaker was Martin Luther King III. They have a list of speakers available.

Homeschooling Information Clearinghouse, PO Box 293023, Sacramento CA 95829-3023. (916) 422-2879. Email: hicnews@aol.com This organization works to increase public understanding of and support homeschooling by distributing information about homeschooling movement to news media, government officials, and the public. They publish a quarterly newsletter, *Spotlight*, focusing on practical ideas and advice for presenting information about homeschooling to the public.

HOME SCHOOLS: An Alternative

National Home Education Research Institute, Att: Dr. Brian Ray, Western Baptist College 5000 Deer Park Dr. SE, Salem OR 97301-9392. (503) 375-7019. Email: bray@wbc.edu This organization, founded by Dr. Brian Ray, produces quality research on home education, and serves as a clearinghouse of research for home educators, researchers, and policymakers. They have a video, *What Research Says About Home Schooling*, ($24) that describes the facts concerning homeschooling. They have been publishing the quarterly academic research journal, *HomeSchool Researcher*. The publication is $25 a year.

ALASKA

Alaska Private & Home Education Association (APHEA), PO Box 141764, Anchorage AK 99514. (907) 696-0641. Publishes a newsletter and hosts events.

ARIZONA

Arizona Families for Home Education, PO Box 4661, Scottsdale AZ 85161-4661. (602) 941-3938. Membership to this organization ($25 family) includes: information packet notes on Arizona homeschooling laws and lists of resources, research and voting information, free curriculum fair and convention admission. The annual Home Educator's Convention and Curriculum Fair is held in May or June.

CALIFORNIA

California Home Educators, 10489 Sunland Blvd., PO Box 4070, Sunland CA 91040. (818) 898-0180. Toll-free 1-800-525-4419. FAX (818) 951-5963. Email: aq483@lafn.org This support group holds an annual curriculum convention. They also have a quarterly homeschooling publication, *Educating Our Children.* They offer legal defense membership for $25 per family per year, have a home school radio broadcast, and have other administrative services for Independent Study Programs.

Christian Home Educator's Association, PO Box 2009. Norwalk, CA 90651-2009. (310) 864-3747. Toll-free 1-800-564-CHEA. Publish the magazine, *The Parent Educator Magazine* for members.

Home School Association of California, PO Box 2442, Atascadero CA 93423. Founded in 1987 as the Northern California Homeschool Association, this organization supports and promotes homeschooling by providing information, monitoring legislation, and conducting an annual convention in Sacramento.

Sacramento Council of Parent Educators (SCOPE), PO Box 163178, Sacramento CA 95816. Phone or FAX (916) 368-0401. This support group offers the newsletter, *Scope News,* meetings, work shops, curriculum fairs, speakers, library, and advertises for businesses that have a Christian or homeschooling focus. SCOPE subscribers are able to take advantage of the SCOPE library which offers books, software, videos and audio materials.

COLORADO

Christian Home Educators of Colorado, 1015 S. Gaylord St #226, Denver CO 80209. (303) 388-1888. (303) 777-1022. This is a support group that has an annual convention, a quarterly newsletter, a resource list, a support group directory, and information on Colorado Home School Law. Volunteers and donations are welcome.

DELAWARE

Delaware Home Education Association, 11 Bristol Knoll Rd., Newark, DE 19711. (302) 633-8528 FAX (302) 993-5950.They publish *Tri-State Network Newsletter.*

IDAHO

Idaho Home Educators, Box 1324, Meridian ID 83680-1324. (208) 482-7336. This group has a June curriculum swap and a spring curriculum workshop. The group publishes *The Bulletin* that pertains of news for home educators of southwestern Idaho.

INDIANA

Fort Wayne Area Home Schools,PO Box 12954, Fort Wayne IN 46866-2954. (219) 483-2807. A support group that sponsors an annual curriculum fair.

KENTUCKY

Christian Home Educators of Kentucky, 691 Howardstown Road, Hodgenville KY 42748. (502) 358-9270. Annual home school convention in Louisville, KY.

LOUISIANA

Christian Home Educators Fellowship of Louisiana (CHEF), PO Box 74292, Baton Rouge LA 70784-4292. (504) 775-9709. Holds a homeschool convention and book fair with nationally known speakers. Getting Started Packet $10.

MAINE

Homeschoolers of Maine, HC 62 Box 24, Hope ME 04847. (207) 763-4251. Is a local support group for Maine residents.

MICHIGAN

Great Lakes Christian Educators' Convention, 8585 Dixie Hwy, Clarkston MI 48348. (810) 625-2311. Support groups that hold an annual Great Lakes Christian Educators' Convention with participating states of Michigan, Ohio, Illinois, Indiana and Wisconsin.

Home School Support Network of Michigan, PO Box 2457, Riverview MI 48192. (313) 284-1249. This organization works to encourage and equip parents in educating their own children. They provide information through their newspaper, *Home Educators' Family Times,* and hold an annual Detroit Regional Home Education Conference which has a curriculum fair, a used book sale, and training workshops.

MINNESOTA

Minnesota Association of Christian Home Educators, (MACHE), PO Box 32308, Fridley MN 55432-0308. (612) 717-9070. This group has an annual curriculum fair and convention in the spring in the St. Paul Civic Center, St. Paul, MN. There are almost 800 active members.

NEVADA

Home Schools United—Vegas Valley. PO Box 93564, Las Vegas NV 89193. (702) 870-5582. Newsletter is $15 for 12 monthly issues. Offers testing services.

NEW JERSEY

Unschoolers Network, 2 Smith St., Farmingdale NJ 07727. (908) 938-2473.

NORTH DAKOTA

North Dakota Home School Association, 4007 N. State St., Rt. 5, Box 9, Bismarck

ND 58501. (701) 223-4080. This is a support group that holds an annual home school convention in Bismarck, North Dakota, publishes a monthly newsletter, and lobbies during the legislative session.

OKLAHOMA

Oklahoma Central Home Educators Association, (OCHEC), PO Box 270601, Oklahoma City OK 73137. (405) 521-8439. Support group that hold an annual convention in Oklahoma City.

OREGON

Christian Home Education Support Services of Oregon, PO Box 13693, Portland OR 97213-0693. (503) 784-4398. Produces the Northwest Curriculum Exhibition, an annual display in Portland, Oregon, of materials that exhibit Christian principles. Exhibitors are by invitation only.

TENNESSEE

Tennessee Home Education Association, Smoky Mountain Chapter, c/o Robert and Sherry Ward, 103 Moss Road, Oak Ridge TN 37830. (615) 482-6857. Support group that holds an annual Educational Resources Fair in Knoxville, Tennessee.

TEXAS

Christian Home Education Association of Austin, PO Box 141998, Austin TX 78714-1998. (512) 450-0070. Support meetings, organization library, annual bookfair/ convention, social activities, seminars such as "How do I begin?" *Newsletter CHEA of Austin* publishes notices of meetings, announcements, and events.

Southeast Texas Home School Association, 4950 FM 1960 W., Suite C3-87, Houston TX 77069. (713) 370-8787. The service area for this homeschooling area has been broadening to include the entire Gulf Coast region of the United States. They hold an Annual Home School Conference in the summer. It is SETHA's purpose to bring praise and glory to God by providing information and support to home school families and others interested in home schooling.

Texas Home School Coalition, PO Box 6982, Lubbock TX 79493 (806) 797-4927. Publishes a newsletter called *The Alert*, for $25.00 per year.

VIRGINIA

Home Educators Association of Virginia, 1900 Byrd Avenue, Suite 201, PO Box 6745, Richmond VA 23230. (804) 288-1608. FAX (804) 288-6962. This support group has a newsletter, *The Virginia Home Educator*, (available to members and membership is $25 per year), an annual convention in Richmond, and a list of resources. One handy resource is *The Virginia Home School Manual*, available from them for $22.50 (member price).

WEST VIRGINIA

West Virginia Home Educators Association, (WVHEA), PO Box 3707, Charleston VA 25337-3707. Toll-free 1-800-736-9843 (WVHE). This group has an annual spring family day, a fall fair, a handbook, and testing services.

WYOMING

Homeschoolers of Wyoming, 339 Bicentennial Court, Powell WY 82435. (307) 754-3271. This group has a state newsletter, county contacts who pass on important happenings and legislative updates, a fine arts fair, and a convention.

BIBLIOGRAPHY

Alternatives in Education, a newsletter. Rt 3, Box 305, Chloe WV 25235. October 1983/ February 1984.

Bandura, Albert with Dorothea M. Ross and Sheila M. Ross. "Imitation of film-mediated aggressive models. *Journal of Abnormal and Social Psychology.* 1963. Volume 66: pages 3-11.

Bandura, Albert. *Social Learning Theory.* Englewood Cliffs, NJ: Prentice-Hall, 1977.

Berger, Kathleen Stassen. *The Developing Person.* NY: Worth Publishers, 1980.

Blinderman, Abraham. *American Writers on Education Before 1865.* Boston: Wayne Pub, 1975.

Blumenfeld, Samuel. *Alphaphonics.* Boise ID: The Paradigm Company.

Blumenfeld, Samuel. *How to Tutor.* Boise ID: The Paradigm Company.

Blumenfeld, Samuel. *Is Public Education Necessary?* Boise ID: The Paradigm Company.

Blumenfeld, Samuel. *NEA: Trojan Horse in American Education.* Boise ID: The Paradigm Company.

Blumenfeld, Samuel. *The New Illiterates.* Boise ID: The Paradigm Company.

Bolmeier, Edward C. *Legal Limits of Authority Over the Pupil.* Charlottesville, VA: The Michie Co.

Burron, Arnold with John Eidsmoe & Dean Turner. *Classrooms in Crisis.* Denver, CO: Accent Books, 1985.

Cartner, Alan with Colin Greer and Frank Riseman, editors. *After deschooling, what?* NY: Harper & Row, 1973.

Clinton, Hillary Rodham. *It Takes a Village.* New York: Simon & Schuster, 1996.

Coons, John E. with Stephen D. Sugarman. *Education by Choice: The Case for Family Control.* Los Angeles, CA: University of California Press.

Cremin, Lawrence A. *The Transformation of the School.* NY: Alfred A. Knopf, 1961.

Duckworth, Eleanor. "The having of wonderful ideas." *Harvard Educational Review,* 1972. Volume 42, pages 217-231.

Edwards, Newton. *The Courts and the Public Schools.* Chicago: University of Chicago Press.

Elkind, David. *Children & Adolescents: Interpretive Essays on Jean Piaget.* NY: Oxford University Press, 1974.

Evans, Richard I. *Jean Piaget: The Man and His Ideas.* NY: EP Dutton & Company, 1973.

Gabler, Mel & Norma. *What Are They Teaching Our Children?* Wheaton IL: Victor Books, 1985.

Gallup Poll. *Phi Delta Kappan.* Volume 62: pages 33-46.

Gesell, Arnold with Louis Bates and Frances Ilg. *The Child From Five to Ten.* (Revised Edition) NY: Harper & Row, 1977.

Gow, Kathleen M., PhD. *Yes, Virginia, There is Right and Wrong.* Wheaton IL: Tyndale House Publishers, 1985.

Growing Without Schooling, a newsletter, 729 Boylston St, Boston MA 02116.

Gustavsen, Gunnar Arvid. "Selected Characteristics of Home Schools and Parents Who Operate Them." (Doctoral dissertation) 1981, Andrews University, Berrien Springs, Michigan. Available through University Microfilms International, Ann Arbor MI.

Gutek, Gerald L., editor. *Standard Education Almanac.* Chicago: Professional Publications, 1984.

Harrocks, John E. *Psychology of Adolescence: Behavior and Development.* Boston: Houghton-Mifflin, 1969.

Hendrickson, Borg. *Home School: Taking the First Step*, revised edition. Sitka, AK: Mountain Meadow Press, 1994.

Holt, John. *Escape from Childhood.* NY: EP Dutton & Co, 1974.

Holt, John. *Freedom and Beyond.* NY: EP Dutton & Co, 1972.

Holt, John. *How Children Fail.* NY: Dell, 1964.

Holt, John. *How Children Learn.* NY: Dell, 1967.

Holt, John. *Instead of Education.* NY: EP Dutton & Co, 1976.

Holt, John. *Teach Your Own.* NY: Dell, 1981.

Holt, John. *The Underachieving School.* NY: Pitman Publishing Co, 1969.

Holt, John. *What Do I Do Monday?* NY: Dell, 1970.

Ilg, Frances with Louis Bates Ames. *School Readiness: Behavior Tests Used at the Gesell Institute.* NY: Harper & Row, 1965.

Illich, Ivan. *Deschooling Society.* NY: Harper & Row, 1971.

Maslow, Abraham H. *Toward a Psychology of Being* (Second Edition) Princeton NJ: Van Nostrand, 1968.

Mitzel, Harold E, editor. *Encyclopedia of Educational Research.* NY: Macmillan.

Moore, Raymond & Dorothy. *Better Late Than Early.* NY: Reader's Digest Press, 1975.

Moore, Raymond & Dorothy. *Home Grown Kids.* Washougal WA: Hewitt Research Foundation, 1981.

Moore, Raymond & Dorothy. *Home Spun Schools.* Waco TX: Word Books, 1982.

Moore, Raymond & Dorothy. *School Can Wait.* Provo UT: Brigham Young University Press, 1979.

HOME SCHOOLS: An Alternative

Naisbitt, John. *Megatrends.* NY: Warner Books, 1984.

National Commission on Excellence in Education. "A Nation at Risk: The Imperative for Educational Reform." US Department of Education, 1983.

Parent Educator and Family Report, a newsletter. Washougal, WA: Hewitt Research Foundation.

Piaget, Jean. *Judgment and Reasoning in the Child.* Margaret Cook, translator. London: Rutledge & Paul, 1962.

Piaget, Jean. *The Moral Judgment of the Child.* Marjorie Gabain, translator. NY: The Free Press, 1965.

Piaget, Jean. *The Origins of Intelligence in Children.* Margaret Cook, translator. NY: International Universities Press, 1952.

Postman, Neil with Charles Weingartner. *Teaching as a Subversive Activity.* NY: Dell, 1969.

Rosenthal, David with Leonore Jacobson. *Pygmalion in the Classroom: Teacher Expectation and Pupil's Intellectual Development.* NY: Holt, Rinehart & Winston, 1968.

Schlafly, Phyllis. *Child Abuse in the Classroom.* Alton IL: Pere Marquette Press, 1984.

Silberman, Charles. *Crisis in the Classroom: The Remaking of American Education.* NY: Random House, 1970.

Skinner, B. F. *Beyond Freedom and Dignity.* NY: Knopf, 1971.

Skinner, B. F. *Science and Human Behavior.* NY: Macmillan, 1953.

Toffler, Alvin. *Future Shock.* NY: Bantam Books, 1970.

Wade, Theodore E. *The Home School Manual.* Auburn CA: Gazelle Pub, 1984.

INDEX

HOME SCHOOLS: An Alternative

ORDER FORM

To order more books from Blue Bird Publishing, use this handy order form. For a free catalog, write to address below or check Web site: http://www.bluebird1.com

_____ *Homeless! Without Addresses in America*	$11.95
_____ *Home Schools: An Alternative* (4th edition)	$12.95
_____ *Home Education Resource Guide* (4th ed.)	$12.95
_____ *Heartful Parenting*	$14.95
_____ *Home Business Resource Guide*	$11.95
_____ *Dr. Christman's Learn-to-Read Book*	$15.95
_____ *Look Inside: Affirmations for Kids*	$18.95
_____ *Preschool Learning Activities*	$19.95
_____ *Parents' Guide to Helping Kids Become*	
"A" Students	$11.95
_____ *Divorced Dad's Handbook*	$12.95
_____ *Expanding Your Child's Horizons*	$12.95
_____ *Road School*	$14.95
_____ *Parent's Guide to a Problem Child*	$11.95
_____ *Multicultural Education Resource Guide*	$12.95
_____ *Dragon-Slaying for Couples*	$14.95

Shipping Charges: $2.50 for first book. Add 50¢ for each additional book.

Total charges for books:_____
Total shipping charges:_____
TOTAL ENCLOSED:_____

Checks, money orders, and credit cards accepted.
NAME:_____
ADDRESS:_____
CITY, STATE, ZIP: _____

FOR MAIL ORDERS, complete the following:
Please charge my _____VISA _____MasterCard
Card# _____
Expiration Date: _____
Signature: _____
Phone#: _____

BLUE BIRD PUBLISHING
2266 S. Dobson #275
Mesa AZ 85202
(602) 831-6063
FAX (602) 831-1829
E-mail: bluebird@bluebird1.com
Web site: http://www.bluebird1.com